A MODERN ART OF EDUCATION

D1526052

[XVII]

THE FOUNDATIONS OF WALDORF EDUCATION

RUDOLF STEINER

A MODERN
ART OF EDUCATION

Lectures presented in Ilkley, Yorkshire
August 5–17, 1923

𝒞 Anthroposophic Press
2004

Published by Anthroposophic Press
400 Main Street
Great Barrington, MA 01230
www.steinerbooks.org

Translated with permission from Rudolf Steiner's *Gegenwärtiges Geistesleben und Erziehung* (GA 307) copyright © 1961 Rudolf Steiner–Nachlassverwaltung.

Translated by Jesse Darrell, except lecture 6 by Robert Lathe & Nancy Whittaker, and lecture 8 by George Adams. All translations revised.

Revised edition by Anthroposophic Press copyright © 2004 Introduction by Christopher Bamford, copyright © 2004

Publication of this work was made possible by a grant from THE WALDORF CURRICULUM FUND

Library of Congress Cataloging-in-Publication Data

Steiner, Rudolf, 1861–1925.
  [Gegenwärtiges Geistesleben und Erziehung. English]
  A modern art of education : lectures presented in Ilkley, Yorkshire, August 5–17, 1923 / Rudolf Steiner.
      p. cm. — (The foundations of Waldorf education ; 17)
  Includes bibliographical references and index.
  ISBN 0-88010-511-9 (alk. paper)
  1. Education—Philosophy. 2. Waldorf method of education. 3. Anthroposophy. I. Title. II. Series.
  LB775.S7G497 2003
  370'.1—dc22
                                                          2003017769

CONTENTS

INTRODUCTION

Christopher Bamford

Rudolf Steiner's lectures and lecture courses on Waldorf education fill at least twenty volumes. Therefore, it is not surprising that there is a certain amount of repetition in these works. It is the differences that are surprising. These often have to do with *who* Rudolf Steiner was addressing. He spoke differently, for example, to anthroposophists in Germany or Swiss public school teachers than he did to English audiences. The English lectures are especially interesting and uncannily accessible for the obvious reason that Anglo-Saxon, English-speaking culture is closer to us in America than, for instance, German or Dutch culture. Like *The Kingdom of Childhood* and *The Spiritual Ground of Education*, *A Modern Art of Education* has an immediacy and intimacy that makes it one of the best introductions to Waldorf education.

Steiner presented the lectures printed here in England in 1923, his sixth visit. He had first come to London for Theosophical Society congresses in 1902, 1903, and 1905, but did not return again until May 1913, after the split with Theosophy. When he did so it was at the request of the newly formed English anthroposophical group. He spoke then on two topics: "Occult Science and Occult Development" and "Christ at the Time of the Mystery of Golgotha and Christ in the Twentieth Century." These important lectures have exceptional liveliness and depth, indicative of Steiner's respect for honest British "matter-of-factness," which demanded that topics be broached head on and without prevarication. He clearly enjoyed the freedom this offered. There was no need for long-winded introductions. The Great War, and its chaotic aftermath, then intervened to make travel impossible.

As a result, Steiner was not able to cross the Channel again until 1922, when he gave several lectures and courses, including the education lectures published as *The Spiritual Ground of Education*, given at Oxford university and hosted by Professor Millicent MacKenzie of University College, Cardiff. As a consequence of these lectures, Rudolf Steiner was invited to give a lecture course the following year at Ilkley in Yorkshire under the auspices of "The Union for the Realization of Spiritual Values in Education." A number of experienced Waldorf teachers (including Hermann von Baravalle, Carolyn von Hildebrand, and Karl Schubert) accompanied Steiner (they were all on their way to the International Summer School in Penmaenmawr, Wales) and gave demonstrations of the practice of Waldorf education.

We are lucky enough to have Steiner's own report on the event.[1] His lectures, he says, were designed to show "how Waldorf methods are related to present-day civilization." He writes: "On the artistic side, we wanted to show how we have evolved eurythmy out of the anthroposophical movement. In addition, six teachers from the Waldorf school were going to show how they put into practice what was described in the lectures."

On his way north, Steiner observed the industrial and coal mining townships—for example, "Leeds, where unbelievably blackened houses are strung together quite abstractly, where

1. Rudolf Steiner, *Rudolf Steiner Speaks to the British: Lectures and Addresses in England and Wales.* London: Rudolf Steiner Press, 1998

everything looks like a condensation of blackest coal dust, concentrated into the shapes of houses where people have to live." He remarked, "Do you see those thought forms—there you have hell on earth." He concludes, "This kind of experience makes obvious how absolutely necessary it is that spiritual impulses should enter our present civilization."

He also remarks how struck he was by the simultaneous evidence of remnants of ancient, Druidic culture:

> Ilkley, then, is a place surrounded on the one hand by an atmosphere created entirely by these industrial towns. On the other hand, in the remains of dolmens and old Druidic altars lying around everywhere, it has traces of something that reminds one of the ancient spirituality that has, however, no successors. It is most moving to have on the one hand the impression [of the industrialism] I just described and then, on the other, to climb a hill in this region so filled with the effects of those impressions and then find in those very characteristic places the remains of ancient sacrificial altars marked with appropriate signs.

He then describes the course itself:

> Each morning began with a lecture in which I tried to put before the audience the kind of education practiced in the Waldorf school, basing this on the whole historical development of education. My starting point was to describe how, in Greek culture, education had arisen from ordinary Greek life. This showed, I said, that no special method or practices should be invented for use in schools, for schools ought to bring children what is there in the culture around them.

> I do not want to be generally critical about, say, Fröbel's way of teaching little children, but I have to say that it is not right to invent special methods for doing things with children—methods that are unconnected with general cultural life and have not evolved from it. The right thing is for

teachers to have a firm footing in general cultural life, to have a good feel and a good sense for it, so that they can base their teaching on what is there in the culture, into which the pupils will, after all, enter in due course. So I wanted to show how education and educational methods must grow out of our own life, a life, however, which is filled with the spirit. This led to an opportunity to shed light on the Waldorf approach from another angle. What I have just mentioned was the starting point. The actual content of the lectures was then the Waldorf approach as such.... Following the lectures, there was a eurythmy performance by the children of the Kings Langley School, and performances in the Ilkley Theatre by the professional eurythmists who had accompanied us there.... The third element was the contributions from the teachers of the Waldorf school who had come with us.

These teacher demonstrations were "met with the greatest interest." One would have wanted to be there! For instance, Dr. Baravalle's demonstration, Steiner reports,

was extremely moving for one who cares deeply about the development of Waldorf education.... To watch him setting out his geometric ideas in a simple way suitable for children; to follow a kind of inner drama in the way Pythagoras' theorem suddenly arose from a sequence of metamorphosing planes that was both artistic and mathematical; and to watch the audience, chiefly teachers, being led step-by-step without knowing where they were going, while various planes were shifted around until, suddenly, Pythagoras' theorem appeared on the blackboard—this was a most moving experience. The audience of teachers were quietly astonished, their feelings and thoughts involved in an inner drama, and they were so genuinely enthusiastic about such methods coming into schools that it was truly moving to behold.

Readers of Steiner's lectures printed here will also be "quietly astonished" and "genuinely enthusiastic." After an introduction, in which he speaks of reuniting science (intellectual knowledge), art, and morality once again, he turns to the principles of Greek education, in which body, soul, and spirit were still a unity. He then traces the development through the Middle Ages, during which new, evolving elements were added. In our time, he says, we must understand the concrete connection of the spirit with the human being, so that thinking, feeling, and willing can once more become alive. He relates this to the child's developmental stages, as well as the human basics such a sleeping and waking. Then he turns to the specifics of the curriculum: reading, writing, nature study, arithmetic, geometry, history physics, chemistry, crafts, language, and religion. Finally, he turns to memory, the temperaments, physical culture, art, and the actual organization of a Waldorf school—to which this volume is, all in all, one of the best introductions.

SCIENCE, ART, RELIGION, MORALITY

August 5, 1923

First, in response to the kind greeting from Ms. Beverley to Dr. Marie Steiner and me, I can assure you that we deeply appreciate the invitation to give this course of lectures.[1] Essentially, my purpose is to show what spiritual science says about education and to describe attempts by the Stuttgart Waldorf school to apply the educational principles arising from spiritual science. We gladly accepted the invitation to come to northern England, and it gives me deep satisfaction to speak on a subject I consider important, especially since I am also speaking to those who arranged this course and have heard lectures on education from this perspective before. Thus I hope that there is more behind this conference than the determination of those who organized it. And I hope it shows that our previous activities are now bearing fruit.

English friends of spiritual science were with us at a conference during Christmas before last, when the Goetheanum—since taken by fire—still stood.[2] That conference was arranged by Mrs. Mackenzie, the author of an able book on Hegel's educational principles, and the sympathetic appreciation expressed there makes one

1. Ms. Beverley was chair of the invitation committee.
2. See Rudolf Steiner, *Soul Economy: Body, Soul, and Spirit in Waldorf Education.* See the bibliography for this and other books cited.

hope that it is not, after all, so very difficult to find understanding that transcends the limits of nationality.[3] What I said about education at that conference did not, of course, emanate from the more intellectual philosophy of Hegel but from spiritual science, the nature of which is wholly spiritual. Again, however, it was Mrs. Mackenzie who discovered that something fruitful for education could be won from spiritual science, which goes beyond intellectuality into the spiritual while taking full account of Hegel.

I was also able to speak of our educational principles and their application a second time last year, in the old university town of Oxford.[4] Perhaps I am justified in thinking that those lectures—which, among other things, dealt with how education is related to society—may have induced a number of English people concerned with education to visit our Stuttgart Waldorf school. It was a great joy to welcome them into our classes, and we were delighted that they were happy with our work and followed it with interest. During that visit, the idea formed to hold this summer course on education. Its roots, therefore, lie in previous activities, and this fact gives us real confidence and courage as we begin these lectures. Courage and confidence are needed when we speak of matters still unfamiliar in today's culture, with strong opposition coming from many areas. Courage and confidence are especially necessary when we try to explain principles that would approach, in a creative sense, the greatest artistic achievement of the cosmos: humanity itself.

---

3. Hettie Millicent Mackenzie, *Hegel's Educational Theory and Practice* (1909), New York, Haskell House, 1971. Mrs. Mackenzie was professor of education at Cardiff University (1910–1915).
4. See Rudolf Steiner, *The Spiritual Ground of Education*.

Those who visited us realize how Waldorf education essentially deals with the deepest fibers of modern life. The educational methods applied there can really no longer be described by the word *pedagogy*—a treasured word that the Greeks learned from Plato and his followers, who had devoted themselves so sincerely to all educational matters. *Pedagogy* is, in fact, no longer an apt term today, because it immediately shows the bias of its ideals, and those who visited the Waldorf school understand this to begin with. Today it is not unusual, of course, to find boys and girls in the same classes and taught in the same way, and I merely mention this to show you that in this respect, too, the methods of the Waldorf school are in keeping with recent trends.

What does the word *pedagogy* suggest? A "pedagogue" is a teacher of boys.[5] We see immediately that, in ancient Greece, education was very one-sided—half of humanity was excluded from serious education. To Greeks, only boys were capable of being fully human, and girls had to remain in the background in terms of real education. A pedagogue was a leader of boys and was concerned only with that gender.

Today, the presence of female students in schools is common, though it is a radical change from not-so-ancient customs. Even today, however, another feature of the Waldorf school will seem strange to many people. Not only are boys and girls considered equal, but even on the teaching staff there is no distinction between the sexes—at least, not in principle—even up to the highest classes. Universally human considerations required us to set aside prejudice. First, we had to give up all that the

---

5. *Pedagogue*, from the Greek word *paidagogos*, a slave who escorted children to school (*Merriam-Webster's Collegiate Dictionary*, 10th ed.).

old term *pedagogy* implied before we could establish an education in keeping with modern conditions. This is only one aspect of the educational prejudice implied by the term. In the broadest sense, it must be said that, until recently, nothing was known of the human being as such in education. Indeed, there have been many biased views in the educational world—not only that of gender.

According to the old principles, once the years of education were over, did "the human being as such" step forth? Certainly not! Today, however, people are preparing to look for this—for pure, certain, undifferentiated humanity. From the way the Waldorf school was formed, we can see that this had to be worked for.

The original idea was to provide an education for children whose parents were working in the Waldorf-Astoria factory, and because the director was a member of the Anthroposophical Society, he asked me to arrange this education.[6] I was able to do this only on the basis of spiritual science. And so, to begin with, the school arose for humanity as such, fashioned from the working class. It was "anthroposophic" only in the sense that the man who first had the idea happened to be an anthroposophist. Thus we have an educational institution with a social basis that wishes to base the whole spirit and method of its teaching on spiritual science. But it was not even remotely a matter of beginning an "anthroposophic" school. On the contrary, we hold that, because spiritual science can always make itself inconspicuous, it can institute a school based on universal human principles, not on social rank, philosophical concepts, or any other particular. All of this may have occurred to those

---

6. The director was Emil Molt (1876–1936).

who visited the Waldorf school, and it can be seen in everything we do there. And it may have led to the invitation to give these lectures.

In this introductory lecture, since I am not yet speaking of education, let me thank those who arranged this course. I also thank them for arranging eurythmy performances, which have become an integral part of spiritual science. Let me begin by expressing this hope: A summer course has brought us together. We are gathered in a beautiful spot in northern England, far from the busy winter months. You have given up part of your summer recreation to matters that will play an important role in the future, and the time will come when the spirit uniting us now for two weeks during the summer holidays will inspire all our winter work. I cannot thank you enough for dedicating your holidays to the study of important ideas for the future. With equal sincerity, I trust that the spirit of our summer course will be carried into the winter months; only then will this course bear real fruit.

Allow me to refer to Miss Macmillan's impressive words yesterday, which expressed a deep social and pedagogical impulse and showed that we must look for profound moral impulses before human civilization can progress further in terms of education. When we allow the significance of such an impulse to work deeply in our hearts, we are led to the most fundamental problems in modern culture—problems related to the forms that our culture and civilization assume in human history. We are living in a time when certain areas of culture, though standing side by side, remain separated. To begin with, we have all that we can learn about the world through knowledge—for the most part, communicated intellectually. Then there is the realm of art, in which we try to express deep inner experiences, imitating divine creative activity with our human powers. We also have the religious endeavors—longings that lead us to unite the roots of our existence with those of the cosmos. And finally, we try to evoke from within ourselves impulses that place us as moral beings in the world's civilized life. In effect, we face four aspects of culture: knowledge, art, religion, and morality. Human evolution, however, has caused these four branches to develop independently, and thus we no longer recognize their common roots. It does no good to criticize these conditions; they are necessary, but they must also be understood.

Consequently, we will remind ourselves today of the beginnings of civilization. There was an ancient period in human evolution when science, art, religion, and morality were united. The intellect had not yet developed its present abstract nature, and humanity tried to solve the mysteries of existence by using a kind of "picture" consciousness. Grand images were displayed before the human soul, and these were passed down to us in a decadent form as myths and sagas. Originally, they arose from experience and knowledge of the spiritual essence of the universe. There was a time when, through direct inner imagination, humankind could perceive the spiritual ground of the sensory world. And human beings made this instinctive imagination substantial by using earthly material to make architecture, sculpture, painting, music, and the other arts. In outer material forms, people embodied the fruits of knowledge to their hearts' delight. With human faculties, people copied divine creation, giving visible form to all that first flowed into humankind as science and knowledge. In other words, art reflected for the senses all that the forces of knowledge had taken in.

In a diluted form, this faculty is revealed again by Goethe in his words, spoken from knowledge and artistic understanding: "Beauty is a manifestation of the secret laws of nature, without which they would remain for ever hidden from us." And again: "Those to whom nature unveils her open secrets are conscious of an irresistible longing for art, nature's worthiest expression."

Such views show that we are essentially predisposed to view science and art as two aspects of the same truth. Humankind was able to do this in ancient times, when knowledge satisfied us inwardly by arising as ideal forms before the soul. The beauty that enchanted could be made available to the senses through the arts, and experiences such as these were the essence of early civilizations.

And the situation today? Because of everything that abstract intellectuality brought with it, we establish scientific systems of knowledge from which art is eliminated as much as possible. It is believed a great sin to introduce art into science, and anyone found guilty of this is immediately denounced as a superficial amateur. It is said that our knowledge must be sober and objective and that art has nothing to do with objectivity, but arises only from one's arbitrary will. A huge gap thus opens between knowledge and art, and humanity can no longer find a way to cross it. But this is our undoing. Whenever we apply science that is valued because it is free of art, we may in fact be led to a marvelous knowledge of nature, but it is nature devoid of real life. We fully recognize the wondrous achievements of science, yet science has nothing to say when confronted by the mystery of humanity. Look wherever you like in today's science; you will find wonderful answers to the problems of outer nature, but no answers to the human enigma. The laws of science cannot approach us. Why? Although it sounds like heresy to modern ears, whenever we approach the human being with natural laws, we must move into the realm of art. Heretical indeed, because people will certainly say that this is no longer scientific. If you try to understand the human being artistically, you are ignoring the laws of observation and strict logic, which must always be followed. However emphatically one may argue that it is unscientific, humanity is an *artistic* creation of nature. All sorts of arguments may claim that artistic understanding is completely unscientific, but it remains a fact that humanity cannot be understood only through scientific modes of cognition. Despite all our science, we come to a halt with the human being. Only when we drop our preconceptions do we realize that we must turn to something else; scientific intellectuality must be allowed to move into the area of art. Science itself must become an art before it can approach the secrets of the human being.

If we follow this appropriate path of development with all our inner forces—not just looking in an outer artistic sense—we can allow scientific intellectuality to flow over into what I have described as *"imagination"* in *How to Know Higher Worlds.*[7] This *"imaginative* knowledge," although an object of suspicion and opposition today, is indeed possible. It is the kind of thinking that is aroused to living and positive activity, and does not passively give itself up to the outer world, which is increasingly the mode of thinking today. The difficulty of speaking of

---

7. The words *imagination, inspiration,* and *intuition* (italicized here) are used here to mean particular levels of inner development. See, for example, Rudolf Steiner, *A Psychology of Body, Soul, and Spirit: Anthroposophy, Psychosophy, Pneumatosophy,* especially the lecture titled *"Imagination–*Imagination, *Inspiration–*Self-Fulfillment, *Intuition–*Conscience."

these things has nothing to do with speaking against the scientific habits of our time. Basically, when one goes into it, one is speaking against all of modern civilization. There is an increasing tendency to disregard the activity of thinking—inner, active participation in it—and to surrender to a sequence of events, allowing thoughts to simply run their course without doing anything oneself.

This situation began with the demand for a materialistic demonstration of spiritual matters. Just consider a lecture on spiritual subjects; visible evidence is out of the question, because words are the only available media—one cannot summon the invisible by some magical process. All that can be done is to stimulate thinking and assume that the audience will energize their thinking to follow what one can indicate only with words. Nevertheless, it frequently happens that many listeners (I am not, of course, referring to those in this hall) begin to yawn, because they imagine that thinking should be passive. They fall asleep, because they are not following actively. People would like everything to be demonstrated to the senses and illustrated with slides or the like, which makes it unnecessary to think at all. Indeed, such people cannot think. That was the beginning, but it has gone fur ther. In a performance of *Hamlet*, for example, in order to understand it we must go along with the series of events as well as the spoken word. But today, drama has been deserted for the cinema, where we need not exert ourselves at all; images roll off the machine and may be watched passively. Consequently, the inner activity of thinking has been gradually lost, but this is exactly what we must take hold of. When this is done, you will see that thinking is not simply something to be stimulated from outside, but an inner human force.

The thinking that is common in our modern civilization is only one aspect of this thought force. If we inwardly observe it—from the other side, as it were—it is revealed as the force that forms human beings from childhood. Before we can understand this, we must activate the inner formative force that transforms abstract thought into images. After the necessary efforts, we reach "the beginning of meditation," as I called it in my book. At this point, we not only begin to transform ability into art, but also raise thinking to *imagination*. We are thus in a world of *imagination*, knowing that it is not a creation of fantasy but a real and objective world. We are fully aware that, although we do not yet possess this objective world itself in *imagination*, we have the imagery of it. Now, the point is to realize that we must go beyond the picture.

There is much to do before we arrive at this state of inner creative thinking. It does not merely contain pictures of fantasy, but images that contain their own reality. Next, however, we must be able to eliminate all of this creative activity; we must accomplish an inner moral act. This is, in fact, a moral act within our being. Once we have taken the trouble to achieve this active, imaginal thinking (you can read in my book just how much trouble), when all of one's soul forces have been applied and the powers of self exerted to their utmost, then one must be able to eliminate what has been gained in this way. We must develop the highest fruits of thinking raised to meditation within ourselves, and then be capable of selflessness; we must be able to eliminate all that was gained. This is not the same as having nothing—never having gained anything to begin with.

Now, if one has first made every effort to strengthen the self in this way and then destroys the results through one's own powers, one's consciousness becomes empty and a spiritual world surges into consciousness. It is then seen that knowledge of the spiritual world requires the spiritual forces of cognition. Active, imaginal thinking can be called *imagination*. When the spirit world pours into consciousness that has been emptied through the greatest conceivable efforts, it does so by way of what may be called *inspiration*. Having experienced *imagination*, through the moral act described we become worthy of grasping the spirit world behind outer nature and humanity.

Now I will try to show you how, from this point, we are led to religion. Let me point out that, inasmuch as spiritual science strives for true *imagination*, it leads not only to knowledge, or to art that itself has the quality of an image, but to the spiritual reality within the image. Spiritual science bridges the gap between knowledge and art. Thus, at a higher level—one more suited to the modern age—the abandoned unity of science and art can reenter human civilization. This unity must be attained, because the schism between science and art has disrupted our very being. Above all, modern humanity must strive to move out of this state of disruption toward unity and inner harmony.

So far, I have spoken of the harmony between science and art. In the third part of this lecture I will develop this subject further in relation to religion and morality. Knowledge that draws creative cosmic activity into itself can then flow directly into art, and this path from knowledge to art can be extended and taken further. It was extended in this way through the forces of ancient *imaginative* knowledge, which also found the way directly into the life of religion. Those who applied themselves to this kind of knowledge—primitive and instinctive though it was in early humanity—did not experience it as external, because, in their knowing and thinking, the divinity of the world lived in them; the creative divine passed into human artistic creativity. Thus, a way could be found to raise physical artistic creations to an even higher conse-cration. The activity that people made their own by embodying divine spirit in physical substance could then be extended to acts in which, as fully conscious human beings, they expressed the will of cosmic divine powers. They felt imbued by divine creative power, and as this path was followed from elaborating material substance to human action, art passed, through ritual, into service of the divine. Artistic creation became service of God.

What is done in a cult represents the consecrated artis-tic accomplishments of ancient humanity. Artistic acts were lifted to become cultic acts, thus glorifying God through matter by devotion to God through the service of the cult. As humanity bridged the gulf between art and religion, religion arose in full harmony with knowledge and art. Although primitive and instinctive, that knowl-edge was a true picture, and as such it could lead human acts, through ritual, to directly portray the divine. In this way, the transition from art to religion was made possi-ble. Is it still possible with our present-day mode of knowledge? Ancient clairvoyant perception revealed to humankind in images the spirit in every creature and nat-ural process, and through human surrender and devotion to the spirit in natural processes, the all-creative, omnipo-tent spirit of the cosmos entered the cult.

How do we know the world today? Again, it is better to describe than to criticize, because (as the following lec-tures will show) the development of our present way of knowing was needed in human history. Today I am simply presenting certain suggestions. Humankind gradually lost spiritual insight into the beings and processes of nature. Today, people are proud of having eliminated spirit from their observations of nature, finally reaching theories that attribute the origin of our planet to the movements of some primeval nebula. Mechanical activity in this nebula are said to be the origin of all the kingdoms of nature, even humanity. According to these laws, which loom so large in our "objective" thinking, this earth must finally end through a so-called death by heat. All the ideals achieved by humanity, having arisen from nature as a kind of fata morgana, will disappear, and in the end only a tomb of earthly existence will remain.

If science recognizes this line of thinking as the truth, and if people are honest and courageous enough to face its inevitable consequences, they must also recognize that religion and morality are also illusions and will never be otherwise. Nevertheless, people cannot endure such a thought, and so they hold on to remnants of ancient times when religion and morality were in harmony with knowledge and art. Religion and morality no longer spring creatively from our inner being; they are based on tradition and are a heritage from times when all things revealed themselves through our instincts, when God and the world of morality were made manifest. Our efforts toward knowledge today cannot reveal God or morality. Science attains the end of the animal species, and humankind is cast out. Honest thinking cannot bridge the gap between knowledge and religion.

All true religions arose from *inspiration*. True, the early form of *inspiration* was not as conscious as that to which we must now aspire, but it was there on an instinctive level, and religions correctly trace their origins back to it. Faiths that no longer recognize living inspiration or revelation from the spirit in the immediate present must make do with tradition. Such faiths, however, lack inner vitality and immediate direction of religious life. This direction and vitality must be regained, otherwise our society cannot be healed.

I have shown how humanity must regain cognition that comes through art to *imagination*, and then to *inspiration*. If we regain all that flows from the *inspirations* of spirit worlds into human consciousness, true religion will reappear. Intellectual discussions about the nature of Christ will cease, for once again it will be known—as it can indeed be known through *inspiration*—that the Christ was the human bearer of a real divine being who descended from spirit worlds into earthly existence. Without suprasensory knowledge, there can be no understanding of the Christ. Before Christianity can once again become deeply rooted in humanity, the path to suprasensory knowledge must be rediscovered. Inspiration must again impart a truly religious life to humankind in order that knowledge—derived no longer merely from the external observation of nature—may find no abyss dividing it alike from art and religion. Knowledge, art, religion—these three will then be in harmony.

Primeval humans counted on the presence of God in human deeds when they made their art a divine office, and when they shared in the fire that can glow in the human heart when the divine will pervades the acts of ritual. And when the path from outer, objective knowledge to *inspiration* is found once again, religion will flow directly from *inspiration* and modern humankind will be able—as was primeval humankind—to stand within a

God-given morality. In those ancient days people felt: "If I have the cult, if I have the divine service, if the cult is in the world and I am woven into it, then my inner being is filled so that in the whole of my life and not only where the cult is celebrated I can make God present in the world."

To be able to make God present in the world—this is true morality. Nature cannot lead us to morality. Only that which lifts us above nature, filling us with the Divine-Spiritual—this alone can lead us to morality. Only that intuition that comes over us, when through the religious life we place ourselves in the spirit, can fill us with real inmost morality at once human and divine. The attainment of *inspiration* thus rebuilds the bridge that once existed instinctively in human civilization between religion and morality. As knowledge leads upward through art to the heights of suprasensory life, so, through religious worship, spiritual heights are brought down to earthly existence, so that we can fill this existence with the impulse of an essential, primal, direct morality actually experienced by human beings. Thus will humans become in truth the individual bearers of a life pulsed through by morality, filled with an immediate moral impulse. Morality will then be a creation of the individual, and the last abyss between religion and morality will be bridged. The intuition in which primitive humans stood as they enacted their ritual will be re-created in a new form, and a morality truly corresponding with modern conditions will arise from a modern religious life. We need this for the renewal of our civilization. We need it so that what today is mere heritage, mere tradition, may spring again into original life. This primordial impulse is necessary for our complicated social life, which is threatening to spread chaos through the world. We need a harmony between knowledge, art, religion, and morality. We need this in a new form—a way to gain knowledge that leads from Earth, through *inspiration* and the arts, to direct life in the suprasensory worlds; then, the suprasensory that we have felt in religion and transformed into volition can once again be grasped and guided into earthly society. Until we see our social problems as matters of morality and religion we cannot grapple with them deeply, and this cannot be done until morality and religion arise from spiritual knowledge. If humanity regains spiritual knowledge, we will be able to do what is needed and link our continuing evolution to an instinctive origin.

We will find what is needed to heal humanity; it is harmony between science, art, religion, and morality.

2

THE PRINCIPLES OF GREEK EDUCATION

August 6, 1923

There is no question that education is on the mind of every soul today. We can see it everywhere. And if we advocate an art of education taken directly from spiritual life and perception, it is its inner nature that distinguishes it from the reforms generally demanded today, not the urgency of its outward appeal.

There is a widespread feeling that the conditions of civilization are in rapid transition and that, for the sake of society, we must heed the many recent changes and developments. There is a growing feeling that children today are very different from those of the recent past, and that it is becoming increasingly difficult for older people to reach an understanding with young people than it was in earlier times.

The art of education I will speak of, however, is concerned instead with the inner development of human civilization. It is more concerned with what has changed the souls of men and women through the ages; it is concerned with the evolution through which these souls have passed over hundreds, even thousands, of years. We will attempt to explore the ways in which, in this particular age, we can reach the human being living within the child. It is generally acknowledged that the successive periods in nature can be differentiated. Just consider the way we take these differentiations into account in daily life. Take an immediate example: the day itself. Our relationship to natural processes changes from morning, noon, and night, and we would think it absurd to ignore the flow of the day. And we would also consider it absurd not to pay sufficient attention to the development revealed in human life itself—to ignore, for example, the fact that an older person's needs are different from those of a child. In the case of nature, we respect this fact of development, but we have not gotten used to respecting the fact of the general human evolution. We do not consider the fact that, centuries ago, human beings were very different from those of the Middle Ages or today. We must come to understand the inner forces of human beings before our treatment of children can become practical and not merely theoretical. We must investigate inwardly the ruling forces in human beings today.

The principles of Waldorf education—as it may be called—are, thus, in no way revolutionary. Waldorf education fully recognizes all that is great and noteworthy in the great achievements of educators everywhere during the nineteenth century. There is no desire to throw out everything and think that everything must be radically new. Rather, the goal is to investigate the inner forces ruling in human nature today, so that we can take them into account in education and thus find a true place in society for the human being in body, soul, and spirit. As we shall see in the course of these lectures, education has always been a concern of society, and it remains so today. And it must also be a social concern in the future. In education, therefore, there must be an understanding of what society demands of any given era.

First of all, I want to describe, in three stages, the development of education in the West. The best way to do this is to consider the educational ideals of the various ages— the ideals of those who wanted to rise to the highest level of human existence, a stage from which they could render the most useful service to humankind. Thus, it will help to go back to the earliest of those ages that survive as cultural influences in the present time. Nobody today can dispute the living influence of the Greek civilization in all human aims and aspirations. So, the fundamental question for educators is: "How did the Greeks try to raise human beings to the level of perfection?" We must consider the progress of successive eras in relation to this process of perfection—the education of the human being.

First, let's look at the Greek ideal for a teacher—that is, the ideal for those who wanted to develop to the highest stage of humanity not only for their own sake, but also to be able to help others along the right path. The Greek ideal of education was the gymnast. Gymnasts were those who had completely harmonized their bodily nature with, to the extent considered necessary, the qualities of soul and spirit. Gymnasts were those who could express the divine beauty of the world through the beauty of their own bodies, and also bring the divine beauty of the world into bodily expression in the child; they were the ones who upheld Greek civilization.

Through a feeling of modern superiority, it is easy to belittle the gymnasts' manner of education, based as it was on bodily nature. But this involves a complete misunderstanding of what it meant to be a gymnast in Greece. If we nevertheless continue to admire Greek civilization and consider it the highest ideal to be imbued with Greek culture, it will help to remember also that the Greeks were not concerned primarily with developing "spirituality" in human beings. Their only concern was to develop the human body so that, through the harmony of its parts and modes of activity, the body itself would blossom into a manifestation of divine beauty. The Greeks' expectation of the body was exactly what we expect of a plant: that, if the root has been treated properly, it will blossom on its own under the influence of sunlight and warmth. In our devotion to Greek culture today, we must remember that the bearers of this culture were the gymnasts—those who had not taken the third step first, but the first step: the harmonization of bodily human nature. All the beauty, all the greatness, all the perfection of Greek culture was not sought directly; it was regarded as growing naturally out of the beauty and harmony of a powerful body, by virtue of inner human nature and activity. Our understanding of Greek civilization—especially their education—will be out of balance unless our admiration for the spiritual greatness of Greece is linked to knowledge that gymnasts were the ideal of Greek education.

As we follow the development of humanity, we come to a decisive moment in the transition from Greek to Roman culture. In Roman civilization, we see first the emergence of a cultivation of abstractions that led to the separation of spirit, soul, and body and placed a special emphasis on this threefold division. We can see how the principle of beauty in the gymnastic education of Greece was in fact imitated by Roman culture; but now, the education of body and soul became two separate areas. The Romans still considered it important to train the body, but gradually—almost imperceptibly—this fell to second place. Their attention was directed increasingly toward something they considered more important in human nature: the soul. The Greek training that was related to the ideal of the gymnast gradually changed, in Roman culture, into training the soul qualities.

This continued through the Middle Ages, an epoch when soul qualities were considered higher than those of the body. Now another ideal of education arose from this "Romanized" human nature. Early in the Middle Ages, an educational ideal appeared for the highest classes, the fruit of Roman civilization. It was essentially a culture of the soul, insofar as soul reveals itself outwardly in the human being.

Gymnasts were gradually superseded by another type of person. Today, we no longer have a strong historical awareness of that change, but those who study the Middle Ages intimately will recognize the event. The ideal of education was no longer the gymnast, but the orator, whose main training was in speech, an essential quality of soul. The knowledge of how people can work through speech as orators was a product of Roman culture carried into the beginning of the Middle Ages. It represented a change from purely physical education to an education of the soul, which continued to train the body as a secondary activity. And because the Middle Ages made use of the orator to spread the spiritual life cultivated in monastic schools and elsewhere in medieval times, in the area of education, orators (though called by various names) assumed the place once held by Greek gymnasts. Thus, in reviewing the ideals that have been considered the highest expression of humanity, we see how humanity advances from the educational ideal of the gymnast to that of the orator.

This affected the methods of education. The education of children was brought into line with what people thought of as the ideal of human perfection. And those who can observe historically will see that even modern educational practices, the ways that language and speech are taught to children, are handed down from the Middle Ages, which held the orator as its educational ideal.

Next came the middle of the Middle Ages, when there was a great swing toward honor and respect for the intellect. A new educational ideal of human development arose—one that represents exactly the opposite of the Greek ideal. This ideal gave the highest position to the intellect and spiritual development. Those with knowledge became the ideal. Throughout the Middle Ages, those who could act through soul powers—those who could convince others—remained the ideal of education; now the knower became the ideal. Just consider the earliest universities (the University of Paris, for example) during the Middle Ages. You can see that the ideal there was not the knower but the doer, the one who can be most convincing through speech, the most skillful in argument, the master of dialectic and the word, which now begins to assume the color of thought. We still find the orator as the ideal of education, although the rhetoric itself has become tinged with the hue of thought.

Now, with modern civilization, another ideal arises for evolving humanity—an ideal that is again reflected in the education of children. Education, even in this age of materialism, is still under the influence of this ideal. Now, for the first time, the ideal of the doctor, or professor, arises. The doctor has become the ideal for the perfect human being.

Thus we see three stages in human evolution: the gymnast, the orator, and the doctor. Gymnasts were those who could handle the human organism out of what they considered the divine order and activity in the cosmos. Gymnasts knew how to handle the soul only to the degree that it manifested physically in the body. A gymnast trains the body and, through it, the soul and spirit, to the heights of Greek civilization. The orator was concerned with the soul and attained a crown and glory as the speaker of soul matters, as a church orator. And finally, we see how the ability to act is no longer valued. Those who only know and no longer work with the soul's nature in its physical activity, but only what rules invisibly in one's inner being, became the ideal of the highest level of education. This, however, is reflected in the most elementary principles of education; it was the gymnasts in Greece who also educated children. Later, it was the orators who educated children. Finally, in more modern times, just as materialism was arising in civilization, it was the professors who educated children. Thus, physical education developed into rhetorical soul education, and this in turn developed into professorial education. Modern education is the result of the doctoral ideal, and those who want to understand the deepest principles of modern education must carefully observe what was introduced through this doctoral ideal.

Along with this, a new ideal has emerged to become more and more prominent today: the ideal of the "universal human." The doctoral education was being crammed even into very young children, since it was doctors who wrote the textbooks and invented the methods of education. Now there is a longing to educate the whole human being, the universal human. Those today who discern things from a basic, elementary feeling for human nature want to have a say in matters of education. For inner reasons, the question of education today has become a problem of our time. We must keep this inner stream of human evolution in mind if we want to understand the present age, because any true development of education must do nothing less than supersede this "professorial" principle. If I were to briefly summarize one aspect of the goal of Waldorf education, I would say (of course, merely in a preliminary sense) that we are trying to turn this "professorial" education into an education of the whole human being.

We cannot understand the essential nature of Greek education—which continues to develop even today—unless we look in the right light at the course of human evolution going back to the Greeks. Their civilization was really a continuation, or offshoot, of Eastern civilization. All that had developed over thousands of years in human evolution in Asia was finally expressed in Greece, especially, I believe, in Greek education. Then, that decisive moment in evolution—the transition to Roman culture—occurred. Roman culture is the source of all that flowed into Western civilization later on, even America.

We cannot understand, therefore, the essence of Greek education unless we have the correct concept of Eastern development as a whole. Those who stood by the cradle of the civilization—out of which arose the wonderful Vedas and Vedanta—would have considered it completely ridiculous that people would sit and study books to pass examinations, hoping to attain the highest development of human nature. It would have made no sense to think that after years, if one is industrious (or months if one is lazy), one could become a perfected human being by maltreating (*training* is not the right word) something vaguely called "the human spirit"—only to be asked how much one "knows."

We cannot understand the development of human civilization unless we occasionally pause to consider how the ideal of one era appears to another. What steps were taken by those of the ancient East who wished to attain the sublime culture offered in the previous age that had inspired the Vedas? What they practiced was basically a kind of physical education. If it was in their destiny, they hoped to attain the crown of human life, the most sublime spirituality, through a cult of the body—one-sided though this might seem today. Thus, instead of reading books and maltreating an abstract "spirit," an exceedingly delicate culture of the body was adopted as the highest educational method in the ancient East. For example, this refined physical education involved a specific and vigorous system of regulating the breath. When we breathe—as indeed we must if we are to get enough oxygen from minute to minute—the process is generally unconscious. We breathe unconsciously. The ancient East made this breathing process—which is essentially a bodily function—into a conscious process. They would breathe in, hold it, and breathe out, all according to a specific rule. While doing this, they arranged their bodies in a certain way. The legs and arms had to be held in certain positions—that is, the path of one's breath through the physical organism when it reached the knee, for instance, had to turn in a horizontal direction. Those who reached for human perfection sat with their legs crossed beneath them. If they wished to experience spiritual revelation, they had to achieve it by training the body, which involved the human air processes, or, in any case, involved one's bodily nature.

What is the basis of this kind of education? The flower and fruit of a plant exist in the root, and if the root receives proper care, both flower and fruit will develop properly with sunlight and warmth. Likewise, soul and spirit live in human bodily nature, the body created by God. If we take hold of the body's roots—knowing that divinity lives there—and develop them correctly, surrendering to the life that is freely developing, then the soul and spirit in those roots develop, as do the inner forces of a plant, which pour from the root and develop in the warmth of sunlight.

To those of the ancient East, abstract development of spirit would have seemed no different than, say, hiding a plant from the sunlight, perhaps placing it in a cellar to grow under electric light, because one did not consider the free light of the sun good enough. The fact that those of the East looked only to bodily nature was rooted deeply in their whole view of humanity. Of course, this bodily development later became one-sided; it had already done so in the Hebrew culture, but that very one-sidedness shows us that they universally viewed body, soul, and spirit as one. Here on earth, between birth and death, we must look for soul and spirit in the body.

It may come as a surprise to look at ancient Eastern spirituality in this light, but when we study the true course of human evolution, we find that the highest attainments of civilization were achieved in times when people could still perceive soul and spirit completely within the body. This was a very significant development for the core being of human civilization. Why were those of the East justified in striving for spirit through methods based on the physical human body—for it must be remembered that their main concern was a quest for spirit? They were justified because their philosophy opened their eyes not just to the earthly, but also to the suprasensory world. They knew that, if you consider the soul and spirit on earth to be independent, it is like seeing them (forgive this rather trivial analogy) as a "plucked hen"—an incomplete hen. Our idea of soul and spirit would have seemed analogous to a hen with its feathers plucked, for they knew soul and spirit; they knew the reality of what we seek in other worlds. They had a concrete, suprasensory perception of it. They considered it proper to look for the human being through physical, bodily revelation, because their basic conviction was that in other worlds, the "plucked hen," the naked soul, is again endowed with spiritual "feathers" once it reaches the proper place.

It was the very spirituality of their worldview that, when considering human evolution on earth, prompted those of the East to bear in mind that, resting within the physical body in a most wonderful way, soul and spirit is within the body when we are born as purely physical beings. They knew that, when our physicality is handled in a truly spiritual way, soul and spirit reveals itself. This was the keynote of their education, including that of the sages of the East. It was a belief that was handed down to Greek culture, an offshoot of Eastern civilization. Now we understand why the Greeks—who brought the Eastern view to its ultimate expression—adopted, even for the young, their own way of training human beings. It was the result of Eastern influence. Attention to bodily nature in Greek civilization simply represents what they became by colonizing the East and by what they received from Egypt. This is how they derived their whole mode of existence.

When we look at the Greek arenas in which gymnasts worked, in their activities we see a continuation of the development that the East worked toward—from a deeply spiritual view—as the being who would reach the highest ideal of human perfection on earth. Those of the East would have never considered a lopsided development of soul or spirit to be the ideal of human perfection. The education that has become the ideal of later times would have appeared to deaden what the Gods had given to humanity for life on earth. And, basically, this was also the view of the Greeks.

It is strange to realize how Greek spiritual culture—which we still think of as so sublime—was regarded then by non-Greeks. A traditional anecdote tells us that a barbarian prince once went to Greece, visited the places of education, and spoke with one of the most famous gymnasts. The barbarian prince said, "I fail to understand your ridiculous practices! First you rub these young men with oil, a symbol of peace, then you throw sand over them, as if preparing them for a peaceful ceremony, and then they begin to rush around as though insane, seizing and springing at one another. One knocks the other down or hits him on the chin so hard that his shoulders have to be shaken to prevent him from suffocating. I do not understand such a performance, and it is certainly of no use to anyone."

In spite of this, however, the spiritual glory of Greece derived from what the prince believed to be such barbarism. The gymnast only smiled at the barbarian, who did not understand how the body must be trained in order to manifest the spirit. Similarly, if those Greeks could see our usual methods of education (which date from earlier times), which speak abstractly of soul and spirit, they would laugh at the barbarism that has developed since the days of Greece. They would say, "This is like a plucked hen. You have taken away the feathers!" The Greeks would have considered it barbaric that children do not wrestle and attack one another. But the barbarian prince saw no meaning or purpose in Greek education. By studying human evolution and by observing what was valued in other eras, we can acquire a basis on which to value things in our own time.

Now, let us turn to the places where the Greek gymnasts taught the youths entrusted to them in the seventh year of life. Of course, what we find there differs essentially from, say, the nineteenth-century national educational ideal. What I have to say here does not hold true for any particular nation, but for all civilized nations. When we turn to a place in Greece where young people were educated from the seventh year of life on, what we see—if properly imbued with modern impulses—affords us a real foundation for understanding what we need in education today. They were trained (here *trained* is used in its highest sense) both in an "orchestric" way and in a "palestric" way. Orchestric, to the outer eye, was an entirely physical exercise—a kind of concerted dance, but arranged in a very special and complex way. The children learned to move in a definite form according to measure, beat, and rhythm, completely in keeping with a certain formative principle of music. The children, moving together in this choral dance, felt a kind of inner soul warmth pouring through and coordinating their limbs. This dance was experienced by spectators as a beautifully composed musical dance. The whole event revealed the beauty of the Godhead and that beauty within human beings. Every experience of this orchestric movement was felt and sensed inwardly. And, through this, it was transformed from a physical process into an expression of soul, inspiring the hand to play the zither, inspiring the word to become song. To understand singing and playing a zither in ancient Greece, we must see that they blossom from the choral dance. Out of what they experienced in dance, people were inspired to make the strings vibrate, so that they could hear the sound arising from the choral dance. From their own movement they experienced something that poured into their words—and their words became song.

Gymnastic and musical culture predominated in Greek education in the arenas. But the musical and soul qualities they acquired arose from the outer, physical movements, performed in wonderful harmonious form in the arena dances. Today, if we directly perceive the meaning of those orderly movements in a Greek arena—which could not be understood by the barbarian prince—one finds that all the forms of an individual's movements were wonderfully arranged, so that the most immediate result was not the musical element I described, but something else.

If we study the measure and the rhythm that were mysteriously interwoven into the orchestric dance, we find that nothing could have been more healing to the breathing and the blood circulation than these exercises in the Greek choral dances. When do we breathe in the best way? How can we cause our blood to move properly through our breathing? The answer is that children must perform dancelike movements from their seventh year on. Then—as the Greeks said—the children's breathing and blood circulation depend not on decadence but on healing. The whole goal of orchestric dancing was to express the breathing and blood circulation in human beings in the most perfected way. They believed that, when the blood is circulating properly, it works right into the fingertips, and people will instinctively strike the strings of a zither or lute in the right way. This was the "flower" of the blood's circulation. The human rhythmic system was kindled correctly through the choral dance.

As a result, it was expected that a musical spiritual quality would develop in the playing, because it was known that, when a person performs the corresponding movements of a choral dance, the breathing becomes inspired so that it functions naturally in a spiritual way. The final result is that the breath will overflow into outer expression through the larynx and related organs. It was understood that the healing effects of choral dancing on one's breathing would lead to singing. Thus, the crowning climax—playing music and singing—was drawn from the healthy organism trained in the right way through choral dance. Physical nature, soul, and spirit were seen to be united inwardly, an inner human wholeness. This was the essential spirit of Greek education.

Now let us consider what was developed in "palestric" exercise, which is named for the places of education in Greece, since such exercises were the common property of all educated people. What was studied in those forms, in which wrestling was evolved, for instance? We see that the system existed to develop two human qualities. Volition, stimulated by bodily movement, grew strong and forceful in two directions. All palestric movement in wrestling was intended to bring suppleness, skill, and purposeful flexibility into the wrestler's limbs. This system of human movement was harmonized so that the various parts worked together properly and, whatever the soul mood, one could move appropriately and with skill, controlling the limbs from within. Rounding movements into purposeful life was one side of palestric exercise. The other side was the "radial" of the motion, in which force must flow into the movement. Skill on the one side, force on the other. On one side, the power to hold out and overcome opposing forces, to be strong in order to experience the world. Skill, proficiency, and harmony of various parts of the body, along with the development of power, give the ability to freely radiate and express one's being everywhere in the world.

They maintained that, when people harmonized their system of movement through palestric exercises, they enter a true relationship with the cosmos. The arms, the legs, and the breathing developed by palestric exercises were given over to human activities in the world. It was known that when the arm is developed properly through palestric exercise, it connects with the flow of cosmic forces that then flow to the brain and, from the cosmos, reveal the great ideas to humankind. They did not expect the musical element to arise from special musical training; it simply united—usually around the age of twenty—with what was drawn from breathing and the blood's circulation. Likewise, what had to be learned as mathematics or geometry, for example, united with the physical education in palestric exercise. It was known that geometry is inspired by proper movements of the arms.

Today, people do not learn of such things from history; they have been forgotten. What I have said, however, is the truth, and it justifies the Greeks in having placed the gymnasts in charge of their educational institutions. The gymnasts succeeded most in the spiritual development of the Greeks by giving them freedom. They did not fill their brains or try to create walking encyclopedias; they placed the appropriate human organs into the cosmos in the right way. People thus became receptive to the spiritual world. As in the East, Greek gymnasts were convinced that this happened, but in a later form.

By giving you an introductory description of an ancient method of education, what I have really done today is to present you with a question. I have done this because we must probe very deeply to discover the true principles of education today. It is absolutely necessary to get to the bottom of human evolution in order to discover the right way to form questions that will help us answer the question of educational methods today. Therefore, I want to present you with one aspect of the subject we are considering. As we go along, the lectures are meant to provide a more detailed answer suited to the needs of today—an answer to the question raised today, which will be further developed tomorrow.

Our method of study must therefore be the result of truly understanding the great question of education, raised by the evolutionary course of humanity. We must then move on to answers that may be given by understanding the nature and constitution of the human being at the present time.

3

GREEK EDUCATION AND THE MIDDLE AGES

August 7, 1923

When I tried to present the Greek ideal of education, its only purpose was to stimulate the ideas that must prevail in today's educational system. At the present stage of human life, it is naturally impossible to adopt the methods of the Greeks. In spite of this, an overall truth of education can be learned from the Greek ideal, and we must begin by placing this truth before us as it was affirmed in the culture of ancient Greece.

Public education in ancient Greece dealt only with children over the age of seven. Until then, Greek children were raised at home, where the women lived in seclusion from outer society, which was the affair of men. That system confirms a truth of education, without which we cannot really educate, because the seventh year of life is an all-important period of childhood.

The main characteristic of the seventh year is the change of teeth. This is an event that is assigned little importance today. But think about it; the human organism brings the first teeth with it as an inheritance—or rather, it brings the force to produce the first teeth from the organism, and by the seventh year they are worn out. It is absolutely wrong to think that the force pushing up the second teeth did not develop before the age of seven. It develops slowly from birth and culminates around the seventh year. It then produces the second teeth from the forces of the whole human organism. This event is extraordinarily important in the course of human life, because it does not happen again. The forces present from birth until the seventh year culminate with the appearance of the second teeth, and they do not act again in our earthly lives.

This fact must be properly understood, but it can be understood only by observing, without preconceptions, other processes in the human being around the seventh year. Until the seventh year, a person grows and develops according to natural principles. Natural formative forces, the soul, and the spirit have not yet separated from one another in the child's organism; they form a unity until the seventh year. As a child develops the organs, nervous system, and blood circulation, this development also reveals the evolution of soul and spirit. A child is given a strong inner force that produces the second teeth, because everything during this period of life is still interwoven. With the second teeth, this force weakens. It withdraws somewhat and no longer works as strongly from the inner being. Why is this?

Suppose we were to get new teeth every seven years (I will take an extreme example for the sake of clarity). If the organic forces we carry within us up to the seventh year—if this unity formed by body, soul, and spirit were to continue throughout life—we would receive new teeth approximately every seven years. The old teeth would fall out and be replaced by new ones. However, through our whole life we would remain children, just as we were before the seventh year. We would not develop the life of soul and spirit that separates from physical nature. Because the physical force decreases in the seventh year, and because the body no longer thrives so well in a certain sense (the body now produces weaker, more delicate forces from itself), it becomes possible for the subtler forces of soul life to develop. The body grows weaker, the soul stronger, as it were.

A similar process takes place at puberty, around thirteen or fourteen. The soul element weakens to a certain extent, and the spiritual aspects appear. Thus, if we look at the first three periods of life, until the seventh year we are beings of united body, soul, and spirit; from around seven to fourteen, we are beings of body and soul with a separated nature of soul and spirit; and after puberty, we are threefold beings: a being of body, a being of soul, and a being of spirit.

This truth opens deep vistas into the whole of human evolution. Indeed, unless we appreciate this, we really ought not to educate children. Unless we realize the far-reaching consequences of this fact, all education must be considered a fairly superficial matter.

The Greeks—and this is the amazing thing—knew this. To them, it was an unshakable truth that, once a boy reached his seventh year, he should be removed from his parents' house, from the mere natural principles and the basic, matter-of-fact nurturing. This fact was so deeply rooted in Greek society that we do well to remind ourselves of it today. Later, during the Middle Ages, traces of this important educational principle still existed.

The modern rational and intellectual age has forgotten these things, and even takes pride in showing that it places no value on such a truth. Children are usually required to go to school at an earlier age, a year or more before the age of seven. We may say that this departure from such eternal principles of human evolution is typical of the prevailing chaos in our system of education, from which we must extricate ourselves. The Greeks placed such a high value on this fact that all education was based on it. All that I described yesterday happened in order to regulate education in its light.

What did the Greeks see in a small child between birth the change of teeth? They saw a being sent to earth from spiritual heights. They saw a being who had lived in a spirit world prior to earthly life. As they observed the child, they tried to discover whether the body was properly expressing the divine life of existence before birth. The Greeks considered it important to recognize, in children up to the seventh year, that the physical body holds a spirit being who has descended. There was a very barbaric custom in certain areas of Greece. People exposed and thus killed children who were instinctively believed to be mere sheaths, not expressing a true spirit being in their physical nature. This was the result of rigidly adhering to the belief that the physical human being during the first seven years of life is the garment of a divine spirit being.

When children pass the seventh year (this, too, was known in Greece), they descend a stage lower. During the first seven years, children are, in a sense, released from the heavens, still bearing the sheath they inherited, which is then set aside at the seventh year. Not just the first teeth, but the whole body is cast off around the age of seven and, indeed, every seven years. In the first seven years, the bodily sheath revealed to the Greeks what the forces of prenatal life had made of children. Children carry their earthly sheath proper, their first true earthly sheath, only after the seventh to fourteenth years and onward.

I am trying to express these things as they were conceived by the highest type of Greeks. They thought that, if they revere the divine in little children, there was no need to be concerned with them during the first seven years of life. They could grow up in whatever families the Gods had placed them. Supraearthly forces continue to work in them from before earthly life. Once the seventh year is reached, however, it is wise to take responsibility for the development of forces within children.

So how do we approach education if we understand how to pay real reverence to the divine in human beings? As much as possible, we must develop the human faculties that unfold in a child up to the seventh year. The divine power—the spirit's expression in the body—must be developed to the greatest possible degree. Thus, the gymnast had to be convinced of the need to understand the divine power in the human body and the ability to develop it there. The healing, life-sustaining forces that a child brings from pre-earthly existence—forces that have been nurtured in a very basic way up to the change of teeth—must be preserved between the seventh and fourteenth years through human understanding and art. Education thus had to proceed in harmony with the natural being. Consequently, all education was "gymnastic," because the education of the divine in a human being was seen as gymnastic. Such "divine gymnastics" must be continued through education.

This was more or less the attitude of the Greeks toward children. Teachers thought that, if through insight they could preserve the freshness and health of the formative forces that developed up to the seventh year, if they could enable those natural forces to continue throughout earthly life until death, then they were teaching in the best possible way. To see that the child in a human being is not lost until death was the great principle, the tremendously far-reaching truth of Greek education. Greek teachers thought that they should make sure human beings could preserve for themselves, throughout life, the forces of childhood, and that between the seventh and fourteenth years, those forces retain their living nature.

This is a tremendously far-reaching and deeply significant principle of education. Gymnastic exercises were based on the perception that the forces of early childhood do not disappear, but merely slumber and must be reawakened each day. Gymnastic education was meant to awaken those slumbering forces between the seventh and the fourteenth years, to draw out forces that were present naturally during the first period. The greatness of their culture and civilization arose from the fact that the Greeks, by introducing the right education, were able to preserve the child in human beings right up until death. When we wonder at this greatness, we must ask ourselves whether we imitate that ideal? We cannot, because it is based on three facts, without which it is unthinkable.

These three facts must be remembered by modern teachers who look back to Greece. The first to bear in mind is that the Greek principles of education were applied to only a small portion of humanity, the upper classes, and they presuppose the existence of slavery. Without slavery it would have been impossible to educate even a small portion of humanity in this way. This education dictates that part of humankind's work on earth fell to those who were limited to an elementary human destiny and without education in the Greek sense. Greek civilization and education are unthinkable without slavery. Thus, the delight of those who look back fondly

to what Greece accomplished in the history of humankind must be tempered by the tragic realization that it
was achieved at the cost of slavery.

The second fact is women's position in Greek society.
Their lives were withdrawn from the direct impulses at
the root of Greek civilization, and this seclusion made it
possible for a child under seven to be left in the care of
instinctive home life—instinct that was cultivated without any knowledge whatever. Out of human instinct, the
elemental formative forces guided child until the change
of teeth. It was necessary that a child's life until then
should, despite its different character, proceed just as
unconsciously in the environment of the family as the
embryonic life had through the forces of nature. This is
the second fact.

The third is really a paradox to modern thinking, but
we must understand it, nevertheless. The second point—
the position of women in Greece—is easier to understand, because we know from a superficial observation of
modern life that, between the Greek age and our own
time, as a result of what took place in the Middle Ages,
women have attempted to share in society. If we still
want to be as Greek as the Greeks were—with conscious
education confined exclusively to men—I wonder how
small this audience might be if it were made up of only
those men who were allowed to concern themselves with
education.

The third fact goes even deeper, and its nature makes it
difficult for modern civilization to acknowledge. We
attain our spiritual life through active human effort. Anyone who observes the spiritual activities of civilization
will have to admit that, in the most important area of civilized life, we must count on what human activity will

achieve in the future. Looking at all the human labor that must go toward the attainment of a spiritual life today, we are somewhat astonished by the spiritual life of ancient Greece, and especially that of the ancient East. Spiritual life was simply there. The role of the seventh year in life—a fact that modern humanity simply does not realize—was deeply rooted in Greece. (Outer indications suggest its significance, but modern culture is very far from understanding it.) It was one of the great truths that flowed through ancient spirituality. We stand in wonder before that spiritual life when we realize the wisdom and spiritual knowledge that humanity once possessed.

Without being confused by modern naturalistic and materialistic presuppositions, if we look back at early civilization and the beginning of history, we find a universal, penetrating wisdom that guided human lives. It was not acquired wisdom; it flowed to humankind through revelation and inspiration. This is what people today will not acknowledge. It will not recognize that a primal wisdom was bestowed upon us spiritually, and that we evolved it in such a way that even in Greece, for example, there was still a concern to preserve the child in the human being all the way through earthly life. This revelation of primeval wisdom can no longer be found, which is a fact deeply connected with human evolution. A part of human progress involves the fact that primal wisdom no longer comes to us without activity on our part; we must attain wisdom through our own efforts. This is related, in an inner sense, to the growing impulse of human freedom, which is in its strongest phase today. Human progress does not ascend, as is readily believed, in a straight line from one stage to the next. Out of ourselves, we have to attain something today that requires losing the revelation that comes from without and holds the deepest of all wisdom.

The loss of primordial wisdom, the need to attain wisdom by our own effort, is related to the third fact in Greek education. Their form of education may fill us with admiration, but it cannot be divorced from these three facts: slavery, the position of women, and the relationship between primordial wisdom and spirituality. None of these exist today, nor would they be considered worthy of true humanity. We live in a time when we must ask how we should teach children, while realizing that these three facts have been swept away by human evolution. We must observe the signs of the times if we want look into the inner depths and find the true impulse for modern education.

The whole so-called medieval development of humanity—which followed Greek civilization and has indeed come right down to modern times—proved by its very nature that, in regard to education, new paths are required, not those of the Greeks, which were well suited to an earlier time. Human nature had, indeed, changed. The efficacy and reliability of Greek education arose from the fact that it was based on human habit—on what could be built into the very structure of the human body.

Until the change of teeth around the seventh year, human development is related inwardly to the body. One's physical development, however, functions unconsciously. Indeed, only when the faculties work unconsciously do they function correctly—indeed, they are reliable only when skills are implanted in the dexterity of one's hands and accomplished without further thought. Once practice becomes habit, I become secure in what I need to do through my body. The true goal of Greek life was to make one's whole earthly existence a matter of habit in this sense. From education until death, human activities were intended to become habitual—to the degree that it would be impossible not to do them. When education is based on such a principle, the natural forces of a child before the change of teeth can be maintained until the end of life.

What happened when, through historical circumstances, people poured over from East to West during the Middle Ages and established a new civilization in Central Europe and the West—even in America? They assimilated the qualities natural to the southern regions, but they also brought different habits of life with them. As a result, it set up the conditions for a totally different kind of individual human development. For example, human consciousness saw that slavery should end and that women should be respected. In relation to evolution of the individual, it was seen that, between the seventh and fourteenth years when development is no longer only physical and the soul is becoming freed from the body, children were no longer susceptible to the treatment used in earlier times. In effect, it was no longer possible to conserve the forces of early childhood for the ages between seven and fourteen. This is the most significant historical phenomenon since the beginning of the Middle Ages. Only today do we see the powerful forces of that phase after the fourteenth and fifteenth years, when human nature rebels most strongly—indeed, when it inwardly carries the forces of rebellion.

How was this rebellion in human nature expressed? In Roman and medieval traditions, the primordial wisdom that had flowed naturally into the Greeks had to be preserved in books and writings. In fact, it was accepted only on the authority of tradition. The concept of faith—as developed in the Middle Ages—did not exist in very ancient civilizations, nor even in Greek culture; it would have made no sense then. Belief began only when the primeval wisdom was merely preserved and no longer flowed directly into human beings. Basically, this is still true of most people today. Everything of a suprasensory nature belongs to tradition; it belongs to the realm of belief, no longer direct and real. Reality now is nature and the perception of nature, but anything related to suprasensory worlds is tradition. Until the Middle Ages and beyond, people surrendered to such tradition, sometimes believing that they did indeed experience such things. But, in truth, direct spiritual revelation came to be preserved in writing, handed down from generation to generation as a heritage, based merely on tradition. This was the outer aspect.

What about the inner aspect? Let's consider Greece again. Soul faculties developed on their own, because the whole human being acquired life habits whereby the child was preserved in adults until death. Music arose from breathing and blood circulation, intellect from gymnastics. Without being cultivated, a marvelous memory evolved in the Greeks because bodily habits were developed. Today, we lack any idea of the kind of memory that, even among the Greeks, was not cultivated in any way. In the ancient East, this was even more significant. The body was nurtured, habits were cultivated, and memory arose from the body itself. A marvelous memory was the result of the proper physical education.

The fact that we need shorthand notes from lectures to help us remember proves that we no longer have any idea of the Greek means of memory, which in a wonderful way made it easy to hand down spiritual treasures for the common good. Lecture notes would have seemed absurd to the Greeks; memory, the capacity of a healthy body, preserved everything. The soul developed from this physical capacity and perceived primordial spiritual wisdom, which came, as it were, through revelation. Such wisdom disappeared and became mere tradition. It had to be passed from generation to generation externally by the priesthood, who preserved tradition. Inwardly, humankind was forced to cultivate a faculty that the Greeks never considered necessary. In education during the Middle Ages, it became increasingly necessary to cultivate memory. Everything preserved by tradition was committed to memory. Thus, education had to cultivate historical tradition and inner memory; memory was the first soul quality to be cultivated after the soul was freed. Those who remember how important memory has become in our schools can see how rigidly memory has been preserved because of historical necessity.

Throughout the Middle Ages, because it was so difficult to gain access to the soul, education struggled forward unsteadily, like a ship thrown out of balance by a storm. We can access the body and come to terms with spirit, but soul is so connected with human individuality that it is less accessible.

Cultivating enough piety to find an inner path to receive the words of the priests and teachers who preserved tradition was a matter of soul. It requires tact of soul to cultivate another's memory without violating that person's individuality—without subtly suggesting one's own preferences. What was necessary for the soul culture of the Middle Ages was heeded by tactful people as much as it was ignored by the tactless. This was the situation for medieval education: it fluctuated between helping and harming the human soul in its depths. And, much of this medieval education has been preserved even today, though completely unnoticed.

Education during the Middle Ages assumed this character, because, to begin with, the soul no longer wanted to preserve the "child." The soul itself had to be educated. And because of the conditions then, the soul could be educated only through tradition and memory. A person is in a kind of flux between the seventh and the fourteenth years. The soul must function without the security afforded by the physical constitution before the seventh year, and direction is not yet available from the spirit. Everything has a very intimate quality, which requires piety and tact.

All of this affected education, with the result that, for a long period of human evolution, education entered a vague, indefinite path. That period during which tradition and memory had to be cultivated was full of extraordinary difficulties for education. Today we live in a time when, because of the natural course of development, we desire another kind of certainty, no longer based on the unstable ground of the Middle Ages. We see this search for new foundations in the countless efforts toward educational reform today, and knowledge of this has led to Waldorf education.

Waldorf education is based on the question of how to educate in a time when the soul still rebels against preserving the "child" after the seventh year. And, in addition to this, how do we educate now that humankind has lost even the old medieval connection with tradition? Outwardly, we have lost faith in tradition. Inwardly we strive to be free and to face life at every moment without restraint. We do not want to stand on a foundation of memory throughout life. Such is the modern individual, inwardly wishing to be free of tradition and memory. No matter how much certain people today would like to preserve ancient traditions, it simply won't work. The very existence of numerous efforts to reform education shows that we face a great problem. It was impossible during the Middle Ages to educate as the Greeks did, and today, education can no longer be based on tradition and memory. We must educate according to our immediate present here on earth, where we have to make decisions as free beings with the given facts of the moment. How to educate free human beings is a question that has never confronted humankind before.

Greek educators, the gymnasts, aimed to preserve the forces of childhood into the second period of life, from around seven to fourteen. The forces of childhood, they said, must be conserved and remain in a person until earthly death. Gymnasts had to foster, in general, what they could only indicate in children of seven to fourteen as they inherited their natural foundation. They had to learn how to determine this and preserve it through their own spiritual wisdom. Evolution during the Middle Ages went beyond this and led to our present condition. It is only today that one's position in society become a conscious matter. This conscious life can manifest only after puberty, after the fourteenth or fifteenth year. Then something appears in a person that I will describe in following lectures as an awareness of the true nature of inner freedom. Then, indeed, a person "comes to one's self." If, as occasionally happens today, one seems to have reached such awareness before puberty, it is not actually a true, but a clumsy imitation of later life.

The Greeks purposely tried to avoid this in an individual's development. The intensity with which they invoked the "child nature" into human existence overshadowed and obscured the full experience of this moment of consciousness after puberty. One passed through it with one's awareness dimmed by nature. Because of historical course of human evolution, however, this is no longer possible. This conscious urge would break out with elemental, volcanic force after the age of puberty if one attempted to hold it back.

During what we call the elementary school age, between seven and fourteen, the Greeks had to consider the earliest natural life of a child. Today, we have to consider the time following puberty and all that will be experienced then in full human awareness by a boy or girl we have been guiding for the past seven years. We can no longer suppress this into dreamlike obscurity, as the Greeks did, even those of the highest levels—for example, Plato and Aristotle, who therefore accepted slavery as an obvious necessity. Because education obscured this all-important phenomenon of human life after puberty, the Greeks were able to preserve the forces of early childhood into the period of life between seven and fourteen.

We must be able to see the future humanity if we wish to educate correctly. The Greeks were able to rely on instinct, because their purpose was to conserve the foundations laid by nature. As educators today, we must be able to develop intuitions. We must anticipate human qualities if we wish to be true teachers. Essentially, our education must give children between seven and fourteen something they can remember when the awareness I have described manifests—a memory that looks with satisfaction at what we have planted in their beings; it allows them positive feelings when recalling their teachers. Our teaching has been wrong if, later on in life, our students cannot think of us in a positive way.

Consequently, we need teachers who have developed intuition, who take the path leading to the spiritual life attainable by human beings, and who can give children of seven to fourteen all that will cause them in later life to look back with satisfaction. Greek teachers were preservers. They saw what lived in children during earlier life and lay dormant there after the seventh year, and they knew they had to reawaken it. What kind of education allows us to implant something during childhood that will later awaken of itself in free human beings? We must lead education into the future, which today requires a complete change in education. In Greece, education arose through devotion to the nature of children. Education was a fact of nature that played into human life. But, because of the way life as a whole has developed until now, it has worked its way out of its natural foundations.

As schoolteachers, we must recognize that it is time to offer children something to which they can say "yes" later on in life, when they have awakened to independent consciousness. Children must not only love us while in school, but find their love justified later on by mature discernment. Otherwise, education is only halfway, weak, and ineffective. Once we are aware of this, we realize the extent to which education, as a fact of nature that works into human beings, must become a moral fact.

This is the deep inner struggle of those who, from the core of their being, have some understanding of what education must become. This feeling becomes the question of how we can make teaching itself into a free activity in the highest sense and to the greatest degree. How can education become an all-encompassing moral concern of humankind? This is the great question before us today, and it must be answered before the best efforts to reform education can be directed correctly into the future.

﹡ 4 ﹡

SPIRIT'S RELATIONSHIP TO THE BODY

August 8, 1923

Education during any era will accord with the prevailing civilization. The gifts of civilization as a whole can be passed from teacher to child. When I spoke of the Greeks, I said that they knew intimately the whole human being, which enabled them to educate in a way that is no longer possible. Their knowledge of the human being was derived entirely from the human body, which was, in a sense, transparent to them and revealed soul and spirit, insofar as their understanding allowed. We have seen how the Greeks educated the whole human being, beginning with the body. Anything that could not be drawn from the body (as music was, for example) was given to the student relatively late, only after physical education was completed, around twenty or even later.

Today, we have a different situation. The greatest illusions about human evolution are caused by the belief that ancient periods—when humanity was totally different—can be revived. Especially in our present time, however, it is wise to face reality with common sense. Once we understand history, we realize that, just as the Greeks had to direct all of their education from the body, we must now direct ours from spirit. We must find ways to approach even physical education out of spirit, because, whether we like it or not, humanity has come to the point where we must take hold of the spirit as such; we must win spirit as our human essence through human effort. And, right when we develop the desire to educate according to the needs of our time, we experience how little progress our civilization has made in becoming imbued with spirit. Then a longing arises to make spirit increasingly a human possession.

Where do we find, at a relatively high level, the idea of modern humanity possessing spirit? Don't be shocked if I describe this with examples from the height of modern culture. What appears at the top only symbolically, and within the limits of the culture, really prevails in civilization as a whole. In our endeavor to understand spirit, we have only today reached the stage of apprehending spirit conceptually through thinking. Perhaps the best way to understand human thinking today in its greatest scope is to observe modern thought as it appears, say, in John Stuart Mill or in Herbert Spencer.[1] I asked you not to be shocked by the fact that I point to the highest level of culture, because, while Mill and Spencer appear to be merely outstanding symptoms, in reality those "symptoms" dominate every sphere and represent the thinking of our civilization. Thus, when we inquire into how people know the spirit from which they must educate, just as the Greek educated the body, we have to say that people know the spirit just as Mill or Spencer knew it.

Now, how did they know spirit? Let us consider for a moment the idea people have today when they speak of spirit. I do not mean that absolutely vague image that

---

1. John Stuart Mill (1806–1873), English empiricist philosopher and social reformer. He was leader of the Benthamite utilitarian movement and helped form the Utilitarian Society. His essay "On Liberty" is his most popular work. Herbert Spencer (1820–1903) wrote *Education* (1861).

hovers somewhere above the clouds, the one given to us by tradition; there is no real experience connected with that. We can speak only of the spirit possessed by humanity when we observe how people deal with this spirit, how it works, and what we do with it. We have to look at the way people *apply* spirit, not what they have to say about it in abstract terms. Spirit in our present civilization is the spirit that John Stuart Mill and Herbert Spencer have already worked into their philosophies. There it is, and that is where we must look for it.

Now let us consider this "thought out" spirit, because in our time spirit is primarily something thought—a spirit capable, perhaps, of thinking philosophically. But, compared to the real essence perceived by the Greeks when they spoke of humanity, or *Anthropos*, we move spiritually in a "distilled" element when we think; it is extremely rarefied. When they spoke of humanity, the Greeks always had a physical image of the person before them, and this physical human also revealed soul and spirit. This person was in a specific place and time, limited by the boundary of skin. Those who trained a person in a Greek gymnasium covered the skin with oil to emphasize that boundary. One was a wholly concrete entity, existing somewhere in time and formed in one way or another.

And now consider our idea of spirit today. Where is it? What is its form? It is vague; there is no "how" or "when," and no definite form or image. People try to build some sort of image, but look, for instance, at John Stuart Mill's idea of imagery. We think in ideas, which are the inner images of words, and Mill said that, when a person thinks, one idea is followed by a second, and again a third. As one idea links to a second, third, and fourth, the ideas associate themselves. Modern psychology speaks in many and various ways about those associated ideas, calling them the real inner essence of spiritual life. What kind of feeling and perception should we have in relation to our own being if this association of ideas were truly what we have as spirit? We stand in the world, ideas begin to move, and they associate themselves. Then we look back at ourselves and our true nature as spirit in these associated ideas. This leads to an awareness of self that is no different than looking at ourselves in a mirror and seeing a skeleton—a dead skeleton.

Think of the shock of looking in a mirror and seeing a skeleton. In one's skeleton, the bones are associated with one another; they are held together by external means, fixed to one another according to mechanical principles. In our idea of spirit, therefore, we merely imitate mechanics. To those who have a full sense of humanity and feel healthy in a human sense, this idea of spirit is like looking in a mirror and seeing one's spirit made up of bones, because the association psychology described in books sees as though in a mirror. We may always have this pleasure (not in a physical sense, of course), for it arises whenever we compare our modern situation with that of the Greeks. Spiritually, we have this experience repeatedly. We seek out philosophers, thinking they might be able to give us self-knowledge, but they give us their books as a mirror in which we see ourselves as the skeletons of associated ideas.

This is what takes hold of us today when we try to think in a practical way about education and attempt to approach it from the perspective of our culture. We get no indication of what education ought to be. Instead, we are shown how to find a pile of bones and how to piece them together into a skeleton. This is how the typical person feels today. People long for a new education, and everywhere they ask how to educate. But where can we turn? We must turn to the general form civilization has taken, and it shows us that we can build up only a skeleton. Now a "strong feeling for civilization" must take hold of the human being. If our feeling is healthy, we must feel imbued with the intellectual nature of modern thinking and ideas. And this is what confuses people today. We would like to think that the mirror reveals something sublime and perfect; we would like to be able to make something of it; above all, we would like to be able to use it in education, but we cannot; we cannot use this to educate.

So, if we want to have enough enthusiasm as teachers, we must first learn to perceive dead in our intellectualistic culture, because a skeleton is dead. If we saturate ourselves with the knowledge that our thinking is dead, we quickly discover that all death arises from the living. If you were to find a corpse, you would not take it as the original being. You cannot think of a corpse as a person unless you have no concept of a human being. If, however, you have an idea of what a human being is, you know that a corpse has merely what's been left behind; the nature of the corpse leads you conclude that a human being was once present.

If you recognize the thinking that people cultivate today as being a dead corpse, you can also relate it to something alive. Moreover, you begin to have an inner urge to make thinking come to life again and to revitalize our whole civilization. It then becomes possible for something practical to emerge from modern civilization, something that can reach living human beings, not merely a skeleton, just as the Greeks reached the living human in their education.

Let us not underestimate the importance of the feelings a teacher must have from the beginning. The teachers at our Waldorf school were initially given a seminar. It was not merely a matter of following the points of a given program. It imparted a definite soul condition, reconnecting what today's culture values as its heritage with our innermost being. Thus, dead thinking comes to life; disengaged thinking becomes full of character; artificial thinking begins to be penetrated by one's whole being, becoming truly human. First of all, then, thoughts must become truly alive in a teacher.

When a thing lives, something comes of this life. A human being is embodied in space and time, has spirit, soul, and body, a definite form and boundary, and does not merely think; we also feel and will. When a thought is communicated to us, that thought is the seed of a feeling and an impulse of volition; it becomes complete. The ideal of modern thinking is what people call "objective" thinking, which is as motionless as possible and intended to be an undisturbed reflection of the outer world, a mere handmaiden of experience. Such thinking contains no force, and no impulse of feeling or will arises from it.

The Greeks began with the physical human standing there before them. We must begin with a human ideal (everyone feels the truth of this), but such an ideal must not be only a theory; it must be alive and contain the force of feeling and volition. When we think about changing education, the first thing we need to do is to get beyond abstract, theoretical ideals. When we take these into our souls, they cannot become inner feeling and volition or bring human qualities into the physical body.

Thoughts today do not become gestures, but they must become so again. It is not enough for children to take in these thoughts passively; they must guide them as they go out into the world as unified human beings; for we must again educate unified human beings, whose physical education is a continuation of what we gave them in the classroom. People do not think like this now. Their idea of what to give in school is so much intellectual information, something needed. But it fatigues and stresses children, perhaps even causes nervous problems. When people feel that something else is needed, physical exercises are given as an "extra." So today we have two very separate branches: intellectual education and physical education, and one does not promote the other. And we really have two human beings—one vague and hypothetical, and one real, whom we do not understand as the Greeks did. We "squint" when we look at a person, because there appear to be two in front of us. We must learn again to see straight, to see people as unified, whole human beings. This is most important in education.

What we must do, therefore, is to move beyond the more or less theoretical facts of education as it exists today, moving toward an education that is practical in the true sense of the word. From what I have said, it follows that much depends on how we return spirit—which we grasp only in an intellectual way—to the human being, so that this vague spirit with which we observe people will become human. We must learn to see people in spirit, as the Greeks saw people in the body.

Let me give you an example to describe how, through spirit, we can begin to understand the human being right down into the body. In discussing how spirit may be connected with a specific human organ, I will choose the most striking example, but only temporarily. (These matters will become clearer in following lectures.) Let me show you a process that the Greeks, too, considered deeply symbolic and extraordinarily significant in a child's development—the change of teeth. This change, in Greece, indicated the age at which a child entered public education. Try to picture the relationship between spirit and human teeth. It will seem odd, perhaps, that when discussing people as spiritual beings, I begin by speaking of the teeth. Nevertheless, it seems strange only because, as a result of modern culture, people may, for example, be familiar with the form of a tiny germ when they look through the microscope, but they know very little about what lies before them. It is recognized that teeth are needed for eating; this is the first striking thing about them. It is also known that they are needed for speech. Certain sounds are related to the teeth; air flows in a particular way from the lungs and larynx and out through the palate and lips, and certain consonant sounds require the teeth. We know that our teeth serve a useful purpose when eating or speaking.

A truly spiritual understanding of the human being shows us something else as well. If you are able to study the human being as I described in the previous lecture, it will occur to you that a child develops teeth not only for eating and speaking, but also for another purpose. As strange as it sounds, a child develops teeth for the purpose of thinking. Modern science is unaware that our teeth are the most important of all our organs of thought. In small children, before the change of teeth, the physical teeth as such are the most important organ of thought. Children, through their interaction with the environment, spontaneously find their way into thinking. As thinking rises from the dim life of sleep and dreams of infancy, the whole process is related to the teeth pressing through in the head. The forces that press the teeth out of the jaw are also the inner soul forces that now bring thinking to the surface from the unformed sleep and dreams of childhood. A child learns to think with the same intensity as that used to teethe.

So how do children learn to think? They learn to think because they are imitative beings and, as such, are completely surrendered to the world around them. At the very core of their being, they imitate events in their surroundings, including what happens because of the impulses of thinking. And then, to the same degree that thought arises in a child, the teeth emerge. In effect, the force that appears in the soul as thinking is also within these teeth.

Let us now follow childhood development further. Around the seventh year, children go through the change of teeth and the second teeth emerge. I said that this force that produces the first and second teeth was present in the child's whole organism, but manifests strongest in the head. The second teeth come only once. The forces that drive those teeth out of the child's organism do not work again as physical forces during earthly life. They become soul and spirit powers; they enliven the soul's inner being. When we observe children around the seventh to fourteenth years—with particular attention to soul qualities—we find that those soul qualities between the seventh and fourteenth years, especially thinking, were organic forces until the seventh year. They were active in the physical organism, culminating as a *physical* force that pushed out the teeth, and finally becoming soul activity.

These things can, of course, be truly observed only when we press forward to the mode of cognition I described previously as the first stage of exact clairvoyance, *imaginative* knowledge. The abstract, intellectual knowledge of the human being that is common today does not lead to this other knowledge. Thought must come to life from within, and become *imaginative*, so that through thought as such, one can really understand. Nothing can be truly understood through intellectual thinking; its objects all remain external. One looks at them and forms mental images of what is seen. But thinking can be reinforced inwardly and made active. Then *imaginative* pictures fill the soul, replacing abstract intellectuality. At the first stage of exact clairvoyance (as I described it), one can perceive how, besides the forces of the physical body, a suprasensory body is working in us—if you will forgive the paradoxical expression. This is the first suprasensory member of the human being.

Now, what are the characteristics of the physical body? It can be weighed; it tends in the direction of gravity. This is its outstanding characteristic. If through *imagination* we become aware of the suprasensory body, which I call the ether body, or body of formative forces, we find that it cannot be weighed. It weighs nothing; on the contrary, it tends away from the earth in every direction toward cosmic space. It contains forces opposed to gravity, and works perpetually against gravity. Ordinary physical knowledge teaches us about the physical body; likewise, *imaginative* cognition, the first stage of precise clairvoyance, teaches us about the ether body, which is always striving away from earthly gravity. Just as we gradually learn to relate the physical body to its environment, we also learn to relate the ether body to its environment.

When studying the physical body, we look out into nature for the substances of its composition. We realize that everything within us that is subject to gravity—our weight—has weight in outer nature as well. It enters us when we assimilate nourishment. Thus, we gain a natural concept of the human organism, insofar as the organism is physical.

Similarly, through *imagination,* we gain a concept of the relationship between our self-enclosed ether body and the surrounding world. In spring, the force that drives the plants out of the soil toward the cosmos in all directions, and against gravity—the force that organizes plants, brings them into relation to the upward tending stream of light and works in the chemistry of the plant as it strives upward—all this is related to the ether body, just as foods like salt, cabbage, turnips, and meat are related to the physical body. Thus, in the first stage of exact clairvoyance, this thinking that forms a unity and is self-sufficient is related to the ether body.

Until the change of teeth, the ether body is intimately connected to the physical body. It organizes the physical body from within and is the force that pushes the teeth outward. Once the second teeth arrive, the part of the ether body that pushes the teeth out has finished its purpose in the physical body, and its activity is freed from it. With the change of teeth, these etheric forces are freed, and it is with these forces that we begin to think freely from the seventh year on. The force of the teeth becomes less physical than it was while the teeth acted as the organs of thought; it is now an etheric force. This same force that produced the teeth now works in the ether body and thinks. When we experience ourselves as thinking beings and feel that thinking arises in the head (many people do not have this experience unless thinking has caused a headache), true knowledge shows us that the force we use to think with is the same as that once contained in the teeth.

Thus our knowledge brings us close to the unity of the human being. We again learn how the physical connects with the soul. We know that children first think with the forces of the teeth, and this is why teething troubles are so connected inwardly with the whole life of a child. Consider all that occurs as a child is teething. All those troubles arise from the process of teething because of its connection to thinking; it is intimately connected with the innermost spirituality of a child. The formative forces of the teeth are liberated and become the independent forces of human thinking. If we have the necessary gift of observation, we can see that process of gaining independence; we can see how, along with the change of teeth, thinking frees itself from the body. And then what happens? To begin with, the teeth come to the aid of speech. The teeth, which initially had the independent task of growth according to the forces of thought, are now forced down a stage, so to speak. Thinking no longer takes place in the physical body but in the ether body, so it descends one stage. This was happening during the first seven years as well, since the whole process is sequential, merely culminating with the second teeth. Then, when thinking seeks expression in speech, the teeth become helpers of thought.

So, we look at a human being and we see the head. In the head the formative forces of the teeth free themselves and become the force of thinking. Then, pressed down, as it were, into speech, we have all the processes for which the teeth are no longer directly responsible, because the ether body now assumes the responsibility, and the teeth come to the aid of speech. Here, their relationship to thinking is still obvious. Once we understand how dental sounds find their way into the process of thinking, we see the task performed by the teeth—how we use the teeth to make the sounds of "d" or "t" and bring the specific thought element into speech.

I have shown through this example of the teeth—which may seem a bit exaggerated—how we can understand the human being through the spirit. If we proceed in this way, thinking gradually ceases to be an abstract wandering of associated ideas and connects with the human being. We no longer see merely the physical functions in a human being, such as chewing with the teeth or the movements that produce the dental sounds of speech. Instead, we see the teeth as an outer imagination in nature of the process of thinking. Thinking "flashes forth" and reveals itself though the teeth; there in the teeth is the outer appearance of thinking. When we really come to understand the teeth, thought that is otherwise abstract and vague becomes a definite image. We see how thought works in the head where the teeth lie, and how thought develops from the first to the second teeth. Again, the whole process assumes formative boundaries. A real image of the spirit begins to arise in nature itself. Spirit is again creative.

We need more than anthropology, which studies human beings in a completely external way and associates human elements just as various properties of ideas are associated. What we need is the kind of thinking that is unafraid to press on toward the inner being, unafraid to speak of how spirit functions in the teeth. This is indeed what we need, because then we penetrate the human being through the spirit. And something artistic arises. Thinking that is abstract, theoretical, and impractical merely develops a person with a skeletal thinking and must be led into the imaginal. Theoretical observation becomes artistic perception and creativity. One must form an image of the teeth when trying to perceive the spirit working within. The artistic element, then, begins to be the guide to the first stage of exact clairvoyance—that of *imagination*. This is where we begin to understand the true human being. Otherwise, a human being is merely an abstraction in our thinking.

When it comes to education, we find ourselves confronted by real human beings. They stand there before us, but there is an abyss between us, because we are there with our abstract spirit, and we must cross that abyss. First we must know how we can cross it. Our knowledge of human beings today is limited to being able to put on a cap. We do not know how to put spirit into the whole human being, and we must learn to do this—how to clothe human beings spiritually, just as we learned how to clothe ourselves externally. We must learn to treat spirit as we treat the outer garments. When we approach people in this way, we achieve a living educational method.

The period of life beginning at around seven is significant because of all the facts I described. There is another point in earthly life that is equally significant because of the symptoms that arise in life. These seven-year periods are approximate, of course, occurring earlier or later in different people. Around fifteen, when puberty is reached, is another time of extraordinary importance in earthly existence. But the emergence of sexual life is only the most outer indication of a complete inner transformation taking place between seven and fourteen. We have to look at the formative forces of the teeth in the head for the physical origin of thinking, which frees itself at around seven to become a soul function. Similarly, we must look for the activity of the second soul force, feeling, in other parts of the human organism.

Feeling releases itself from the physical constitution much later than does thinking. Between seven and fourteen, a child's feeling life is still inwardly connected to the physical organism. Thinking has been freed, but feeling is still inwardly connected to the body. All the feelings of joy, sorrow, and pain that a child expresses maintain a strong physical correlation with organic secretions and with the acceleration or slowing of a child's breathing. If our perception is sharp enough, when the outer symptoms of the change appear, we can see in these phenomena the great transformation taking place in the feelings. Just as the appearance of the second teeth indicates one climax of growth, speech expresses the end of the next phase—when feeling is gradually released from its connection with the body to become a soul function. We see this most clearly in boys with the change of voice. The head reveals the change that lifts thinking out of the physical organism, and the breathing system—the seat of organic rhythmic activity—expresses the liberation of feeling, which detaches itself from the physical organism and becomes an independent function of soul. We know how this is expressed in a boy. The larynx changes, and the voice becomes deeper. In girls, different phenomena appear in physical development, but this is only external.

Anyone who has reached the first stage of exact clairvoyance, *imaginative* perception, knows, because it is perceived; the larynx of a boy transforms at about fourteen. The same thing happens in girls to the ether body. The change withdraws to the ether body of the female and assumes a form exactly like the physical body of the male. And the ether body of a boy of fourteen assumes a form resembling the physical body of a female. However extraordinary it may seem to a mode of cognition that clings to the physical, it is nevertheless true that, from this very important phase onward, a man carries etherically a woman, and the woman carries etherically a man. This is expressed in different ways in males and females.

If one goes beyond *imagination* and reaches the second stage of exact clairvoyance (described in greater detail in my books), one attains *inspiration*—perception of independent spirit, no longer connected to the physical body. One then becomes aware how, during this important period around fourteen and fifteen, the third human member reaches a state of independence. In my books I have called this third aspect the astral body, according to an older tradition.[2] This astral body is more essentially soul than is the ether body; indeed, the astral body is soul and spirit. It is the third member and second suprasensory member of the human being.

This astral body works through the physical organism until the fourteenth or fifteenth year, when it becomes independent. Thus, a very significant task falls to teachers—to help this development toward independence of soul and spirit hidden in the depths of the organism before the age of seven or eight. Gradually, because the process is successive, it frees itself. We must assist this gradual process of detachment when we teach children between the ages of seven and fourteen. Then, if we have gained the kind of knowledge I have spoken of, we notice

2. You must not be shocked by such expressions; we have to use words for everything. — R. STEINER

how a child's speech changes. Today's crude science (if I may call it so) is concerned merely with the grosser human soul qualities, speaking of the other phenomena as secondary sexual characteristics. To spiritual observation, however, these secondary phenomena are primary, and vice versa. These metamorphoses, as well as the way feeling withdraws from the organs of speech, are extremely significant.

As teachers, it is our wonderful task—one that inspires our innermost being—to gradually release speech from the bodily constitution. It's wonderful to see in a child of seven the natural, spontaneous movements of the lips, which come from organic activity. When a seven-year-old speaks labial sounds, it is different from the way a child of fourteen or fifteen says them. For a seven-year-old, the labial sounds are organic; the circulation of the fluids involuntarily shoots into the lips. When a child reaches around thirteen, this organic activity is transferred into the organism proper, and the soul activity of feeling must emerge and move the lips voluntarily, with the expression of feelings in speech.

The hardened thought element of speech is manifested in the teeth, and the soft, loving element of feeling manifested in the lips. It is the labial sounds that give warmth and loving sympathy to speech. This marvelous transition from the organic activity of the lips to the activity brought into play by the soul—this development of the lips in human organic and psychological nature—is something a teacher can accompany, and thus a wonderful atmosphere can be brought into the school. Just as we see the suprasensory etheric element that permeates the body emerging in the seventh year as independent thinking power, similarly we see the element of independent soul and spirit emerging at the age of fourteen or fifteen. As teachers, we help bring the soul and spirit to birth. What Socrates meant is seen at a higher level.

In following lectures I will explain the new elements that appear in walking and movement when a person reaches approximately twenty-one years of age, the third period of life. It is enough today that we saw how thinking frees itself from organic activity and how feeling frees itself from organic activity until fourteen or fifteen. And we saw how this gives us insight into human development and how an otherwise merely abstract mode of thinking can become an image, or *imagination.* We have also seen how human speech appears in its true form as soul and spirit when a person reaches fourteen or fifteen.

We can say, therefore, that if we wish to reach a person in a living way and bring vital spirit to humankind, we must enter the artistic. And if we wish to bring the feeling spirit to a human being, we must go about this not only artistically, but also with a religious feeling, which alone can penetrate the reality of spirit.

Education between seven and fourteen, therefore, can be carried on in a truly human sense only if it is done within a religious atmosphere, becoming almost a sacramental office—not in a sentimental sense, but in a truly human sense. So we see that whatever we do returns to us when we bring life and soul to our otherwise abstract thinking, which arises from the mere association of ideas. We see how one finds the way to an artistic understanding of humanity and to a sense of the human within the religious life. Art and religion are thus united with education. Thus, the way becomes clear, from the matter of the student to that of the teacher, when we realize that education should become knowledge so practical, so clear, and so living that teachers cannot become true educators of young people unless they are inwardly able to become truly artistic and religious.

FREEING VOLITION
IN THE HUMAN ORGANISM

August 9, 1923

Yesterday I tried to describe the way thinking becomes independent around the seventh year, and feeling around the fourteenth year, thus releasing themselves from the physical organism. Today I want to show how volition gradually presses on toward independence during the growth processes.

The human will remains connected to the organism longer than does thinking and feeling. Until about twenty or twenty-one, the human will depends very much on organic activity, in particular on the way the breathing continues into the blood's circulation and on the way, through the inner warmth that has developed, the blood circulation then takes hold of the motor organization. The blood circulation takes hold of the force arising in the legs, feet, arms, and hands when we move, transforming it into a manifestation of volition.

It can be said that volition as a whole in a child, even up to fifteen and twenty-one, depends on the way in which the forces of the organism work into movement. Teachers, more than anyone else, must cherish the power to observe such things without preconceptions. They must be able to notice when a child is energetic or pre-disposed to an energetic will—for example, when a child walks, whether the heel is placed firmly on the ground. It indicates a less energetic will if the child uses the front part of the foot and has a "tripping" gait.

Even after the fifteenth year, however, this is still all an outer, physical expression of volition—the way the legs are placed, the capacity to prolong a movement of the arms into dexterity of the fingers. Not until around twenty is the will released from the organism in the same way that feeling was released at about fourteen, and thinking around seven with the change of teeth. The outer processes that are revealed by the liberated thinking are very striking and can readily be perceived; the change of teeth is a remarkable phenomenon in human life. The emancipation of feeling is less obvious; it expresses itself in the development of the so-called secondary sexual organs—for example, the change of voice in a boy or the change of inner life habits of a girl. Feeling, therefore, becomes independent of the physical body in a more inner way. The outer symptoms of the emancipation of the volition at about twenty or twenty-one are even less obvious, and thus they are generally unnoticed in an age that lives in externals.

In our day (in their own opinion), people are "grown up" when they reach fourteen or fifteen. Our young people will not recognize that, between fifteen and twenty-one, they should not only acquire external information, but also develop inner character and, most important, volition. Even before twenty-one, young people set themselves up as reformers and teachers, and instead of applying themselves to what they can learn from those who are older, they write pamphlets and that sort of thing. This is understandable in an age that is directed so much toward outer life. The decisive change that occurs around twenty-one is hidden from people today, because it is completely inner. But this change does indeed take place, and it can be described.

Up until sometime around the age of twenty-one, one has not yet become a self-contained personality; one is strongly influenced by the earth's gravitational forces, with which one struggles. Conventional science will discover much about these things, which are already known to the exact clairvoyance I described yesterday.

We have iron within the corpuscles of our circulatory system, and until around twenty-one those blood corpuscles are such that gravity weighs them down. After the age of twenty-one, our being receives a push upward from below, which also affects the blood. From twenty-one on, we place our feet on the earth in a new way. This is largely unknown today, but it is a fundamentally important fact for understanding the human being in relation to education. After twenty-one, with every step we take, a new force works into the human organism from below upward. Previously, our formative forces flowed downward from the head, but at twenty-one, we become self-contained beings, because now the forces that work upward from below have stopped the forces working downward. This downward stream of forces is strongest in smaller children, up to the age of seven. The whole process of physical development during this period begins in the head. Up until seven, the head does everything, but when thinking liberated at the change of teeth, the head frees itself from this strong downward force.

Much is known today about the polar nature of magnetism and electricity, but little is known about what occurs in a human being. The fact that forces flow from the head to the feet and from the feet to the head only during the first twenty years of one's life is a very significant spiritual scientific truth—indeed, one that is extremely important for education. It is a fact that people today are completely unaware of. Yet all education is based on the question of *why* we educate in the first place. This is the grand question.

Because we are human and not animals, we must ask: Why do we need to educate people? How do animals grow up and function in life without education? Why can't we acquire what we need in life by simply observing and imitating? Why should teachers intervene in the freedom of children? People seldom ask these questions, because such matters are taken for granted. We cannot become real teachers, however, unless we no longer accept this as a matter of fact. We must recognize that we interfere with children when we stand before them and try to educate them. And why should children accept it?

We consider it an obvious fact that we must educate our children, but in the children's subconscious life, they do not. Consequently, we talk a great deal about the behavior of children, but it never occurs to us that, to their subconscious, we probably appear very comical when we teach something of the outer world. And they are quite justified in their antipathy. The great problem for educators is how to change an object of apathy for children into something they can relate to. We are given the opportunity to do this between the seventh and fourteenth years, because at seven, the head—the carrier of thought—is liberated. It no longer generates the downward forces as strongly as it did; it settles down and becomes more concerned with its own affairs.

Not until around fifteen does the system of movement assume a more personal quality of volition. The will gains independence from the system of movement, and the forces of will, which flowed upward, now begin to work for the first time. All volition works its way upward, all thinking downward. The direction of thought is from heaven to earth; the direction of will is from earth to heaven. Between seven and fifteen, these two functions are not connected, nor do they interpenetrate. In the central system of the body, where the breathing and circulation originate and take place, one's feeling nature is present, and it frees itself at this time. If feelings are properly developed between seven and fifteen, we establish a true relationship between the downward and upward moving forces.

It comes down to the fact that, between seven and fifteen, we must help a child establish the right relationship between thinking and volition, and here it is possible to fail. Because of this, we have to educate our children. In animals, this interaction between thinking and volition happens automatically, insofar as animals have volition and think in a dreamlike way. In a human being, the interaction of thinking and volition does not occur automatically. In animals, the process is natural; in human beings, it must be the result of a moral process. We can become moral beings because we have the opportunity on earth to unite thinking and volition. The whole human character—insofar as it arises from one's inner being—depends on whether human activity establishes true harmony between thinking and willing.

The Greeks brought about this harmony of thinking and volition through gymnastics, evoking the flow of forces from the head into the limbs (which happens naturally in the earliest years of life) and allowing the arms and legs to move through dance and wrestling. Thus, the head's activity moves into the limbs. We cannot, however, return to Greek culture, nor can we repeat their civilization. We must now begin with spirit. Thus, we must understand how, at twenty-one, the will is freed through inner processes of the system of movement, just as feeling was freed at fourteen, and thinking at seven.

Modern civilization is mostly unaware of this. It is asleep to the insight that education must unify thinking and the will. Thinking was already released at seven, and volition now appears in full freedom as a soul quality around the twentieth year. We cannot acquire true reverence for human development unless we bring spirit into contact with physical human nature, as we showed yesterday with regard to thinking and feeling, and as we have just tried to show with volition. With the twentieth or twenty-first year, we must be able to see the will at work in the organization of human movement—in distinct movements of the fingers and arms and in individual ways of walking. The young person has been preparing for this, however, since the fifteenth year. If we can thus reclaim a sense of spirit that is no longer a mere association of ideas—a "skeleton" of spirit—but a living spirit that can even perceive how a person walks or moves the fingers, then we have also reclaimed the human being, and we can now teach.

The Greeks' power of perception was instinctive, but it was very slowly lost, to be continued as a tradition until the sixteenth century. The most conspicuous thing about the sixteenth century is that civilized humanity in general lost their understanding of the relationship between thought and volition. Since then, people have begun to reflect about education, yet have no regard for the most significant problems in their understanding of the human being. The human being, whom they want to educate, is simply not understood. This tragedy has existed ever since the sixteenth century.

Today, people experience and recognize that education must be transformed. Educational reform organizations are springing up everywhere. People sense that education needs something but fail to arrive at the essential question: How can thought and volition be harmonized in human beings? People might at least realize that there is too much intellectuality—that education must become less intellectual and begin to educate the will. But the will must not be educated for its own sake. And it is superficial to talk only about which is better, educating thinking or educating the will. There is only one question that is truly practical and relevant to human nature: How can we establish real harmony between thinking, which is liberating itself in the head, and the will, which is becoming free in the limbs?

To be educators in the truest sense, we cannot take a one-sided approach; rather, we must consider the whole being, in every aspect. And we cannot do this merely through the usual association of ideas we use to describe spirit today; it is impossible unless we recognize that the prevailing mode of thinking today is merely the corpse of living thinking (as shown in my previous two lectures), and understand that we must work our way toward living thinking through self-development.

In this sense, let me frankly present one fundamental principle of all educational reform. I must ask your patience if I say this too bluntly, because to say it almost seems like an insult to modern humanity, and one is always reluctant to be insulting. It is peculiar to modern civilization that people understand that education must change, which has led to the countless groups advocating educational reform. People know very well that education is not right and that it needs to change. However, people are just as convinced that they know exactly what education should become, that each group can dictate how we ought to educate. But people should consider the fact that, if education is so poor that it must be reformed fundamentally, they themselves have suffered from it, and a poor education may not have rendered them capable of understanding what is right for education. Today, people realize that they have all been educated poorly, but they also assume that they know perfectly well what a good education should be. And these educational reform groups spring up like so many mushrooms.

The Waldorf method did not begin with this principle, but from the fact that people do not yet know what education should be and that we must first acquire a basic knowledge of the human being. Consequently, the first seminar for the Waldorf school involved teaching about fundamental human nature, so that teachers would gradually learn what they could not yet know: how children should be taught. It is impossible to know how to teach without an understanding of the human being.

The first thing we gave teachers in the seminar was a basic knowledge of the human being. We hoped that, by contemplating the true nature of humanity, inner enthusiasm and love for education would grow within them. With such knowledge comes a spontaneous love for humanity that is the very best quality for the practice of education. Pedagogy is a love for humanity, resulting from knowing humanity, and only on this basis can it be established.

To those who observe human life as expressed externally today, all the educational reform groups are only an
outer indication that people know a great deal about how
children should be taught these days. To those who have
a deeper understanding of human life, this is not so. The
Greeks educated instinctively; they did not talk much
about education. Plato was the first to speak a little about
education from the perspective of a sort of philosophical
miseducation.

Before the sixteenth century, people didn't talk a great
deal about education. Indeed, people in general speak
very little of what they can do and much more of what
they cannot. To those with a deeper knowledge of human
nature, too much talk about anything is not a good sign
that it is understood; on the contrary, life reveals that,
when people of any era tend to discuss some subject too
much, it is a sign that very little is known about it. So, for
those who can truly see modern civilization, the "problem of education" emerged because it is no longer understood how human development occurs.

In making a statement such as this, one must of course
ask forgiveness, and I do this with all due respect. The
truth, however, cannot be denied and must be stated. If
the Waldorf method achieves anything, it will happen by
substituting knowledge of the human being for ignorance
of the human being, by replacing mere external anthropology with true spiritual scientific understanding of
inner human nature. This brings living spirit right down
into the physical human constitution.

Someday in the future, it will be no less natural to
speak of human nature with understanding than it is to
speak with ignorance today. Someday it will be known,
even in society as a whole, how thinking is connected

with the force that enables the teeth to grow. Someday people will be able to observe how the inner force of feeling is connected to what comes from the chest and is expressed through the lips' movement. The variations in lip movements and the control of them through feeling, which sets in between seven and fourteen, will be a significant outer sign of inner development. And it will be seen how, between fourteen and twenty-one, the forces flowing upward consolidate and are stopped in the head itself. The quality of thought manifests in the teeth and the quality of feeling in the lips. Likewise, in the significant way that the palate limits the mouth cavity at the back, true knowledge of the human being will see how the upward forces work and, stopped by the gums, pass into speech. Someday people may go beyond looking at the smallest and largest through microscopes or telescopes, and instead observe closely what they see in the outer world—and this is not seen today, despite the tools available. If so, people will perceive how thinking lives in the labial sounds and volition in the palatal sounds (which influence especially the tongue), and how, through those sounds, speech, like every other function, becomes an expression of the whole human being.

There are people today who try to read the lines of the hand and other such outer phenomena. They try to understand human nature according to symptoms. These things cannot be correctly understood unless it is also understood that we must look for the whole human being in what one expresses. People must see how speech, which makes individuals into social beings, has an inner movement and configuration that reflects the whole human being. Dental sounds, labial sounds, and palatal sounds do not exist in speech by chance; they occur because the whole human being enters speech through the dental sounds of the head, the labial sounds of the breast, and the palatal sounds of the remaining human organization.

Our civilization must, therefore, learn to speak of a revelation of the whole human being; then spirit will be brought to the whole human being. A way will be found from spirit into the most intimate expressions of our being: our moral life. From this will proceed an inner impulse for the education we truly need.

The Gospel of St. John is the most significant document that reveals how we must change our worldview and civilization from that of ancient times. It is the deepest and most beautiful document of Greek culture. From the very first line, this marvelous Gospel tells that we must rise to very different ideas—living ideas—before we can learn something from the ancients for our time. In John's Gospel, Greek thought and feeling were a garment for the newly arising Christianity. The first line says, "In the beginning was the Word" (*Logos* in Greek). When we hear someone say "word" today, there is nothing left in our feelings for what the writer felt when writing the sentence "In the beginning was the Word." The feeble, insignificant meaning we give that word was certainly not in the mind of the Gospel writer when he wrote this line. Something very different was meant by *word*. To us, the "word" is a weak expression of abstract thoughts. To the Greeks, it was still a call to human volition. When a syllable was spoken, the body of a Greek would "tingle" and express this syllable throughout one's whole being. The Greeks still had the knowledge that one does not just express oneself by saying, for example, "It's all the same to me." When they heard someone say this, they tingled, prompting them to make a corresponding movement (shrugging the shoulders). Word did not live only in the speech organs, but in the whole human organism of movement. Humankind has forgotten these things.

If you want to realize how word—which in ancient Greece still summoned a gesture—can live throughout the human being, you should go to the eurythmy performance next week. It is just a beginning, a very modest initiative to bring the word back into the will, to show the human being (on the stage at any rate, even if it is not possible in ordinary life) that the word does in fact live in the movements of one's arms and legs. When we introduce eurythmy into our schools, it is a humble beginning (even today) to make the word once more an aspect of movement in all of life.

In Greece, a very different feeling remained, which had come from the East. There was a tingling, or urge, in a person to allow volition to reveal itself through the limbs, with every syllable, word, or phrase, with the rhythm and measure of that speech. The Greeks realized how the word could become creative in every movement. But they also knew more. To them, words expressed the forces of a cloud formation, plant growth, and natural phenomena in general. Word rumbled in the rolling waves and worked in the whistling wind. Just as the word lives in our breath, leading to a corresponding movement, the Greeks found the word living in the raging winds, in the surging waves, and even in rumbling earthquakes. These were words that poured out of the earth.

The paltry ideas that arise in us when we hear "word" would be very misplaced if I could transfer them to the world's primal beginning. I wonder how we might have begun with words and ideas if, at the beginning of the world, our feeble ideas of "word" had been present then, and had been thought to be creative. Our words have become intellectualized; they no longer have any creative power.

Thus, above all, we must rise to what the Greeks felt as a revelation of the whole human being, a call to the will when they spoke of the word, or *Logos*. The Greeks felt *Logos* surging and sounding throughout the cosmos. They could feel what really sounds when one says, "In the beginning was the Word." In all that was conjured up in these words, a living creative force lived not only in humanity, but in wind, wave, cloud, sunlight, and star-light. Everywhere, the world and the cosmos revealed the word. Greek gymnastics revealed the word. And in its weaker expression of musical education, there was a vague image of all that was felt in the word. The word worked in Greek wrestling. The vague image of the word in music functioned also in the Greek dances. The spirit worked into the nature of humanity, even though it involved a physical, gymnastic education.

We must realize how weak our ideas have become, and begin to see correctly how the grand impulse rever-berating in a line such as "In the beginning was the Word" was reduced as it passed into Roman culture, becoming increasingly vague, until we feel today only an inner lassitude when speaking of it. In ancient times, all wisdom, all science, was a commentary on "In the begin-ning was the Word." Initially, the word, or *Logos*, lived in the ideas that arose in people when they spoke those words, but this increasingly weakened. Then came the Middle Ages, and *Logos* died; only a dead *Logos* could be tolerated. Educated people were taught in the dead *Logos*, the dead word of decaying Latin. The dying word of speech became the main medium of education until the sixteenth century, when certain inner revolt arose against it.

So what did civilization mean up to the sixteenth century and the death of human feeling for the living *Logos* as contained in the Gospel of John? The attachment to a dead language was merely an outer manifestation of this death of the *Logos*. If we wanted to briefly describe the course of civilization as it affects education, we would have to say that everything humanity lost is expressed most clearly by the fact that it no longer understands matters such as those in John's Gospel.

The course of civilization, through the Middle Ages until the sixteenth century, lost the inner force of a text such as John's Gospel, and this has led to the inadequacy of humanity today; hence the clamor for educational reforms. The question of education will not get its bearing until people understand the barrenness of the human heart when trying to understand the Gospel of John, comparing this to the intense devotion of those who felt transported from their being into the creative forces of the universe, allowing the real meaning of that first sentence of the Gospel to reverberate inwardly. We must realize that the sixteenth and seventeenth centuries called for a new kind of education because the most godly people, those who most deeply felt the need for a renewal of education, also sensed the loss of the inner elemental life-force that enables us to understand spirit. After all, the Gospel of John refers to spirit when speaking of *Logos*.

Indeed, we have reached a point where we long for spirit, but our speech is made up of mere words; we have lost the spirit of the word. This still existed for the Greeks, and their whole being and activity in the world dawned in them when a word was spoken. Similarly, in even earlier times, cosmic activity dawned in human beings when they recognized the divine spiritual ground of the world in universally creative words. These must come to life in each of us if we are to become completely human. And teachers must become whole human beings if they are to educate whole human beings. Teachers must return to an understanding of the word. But before we can bring the full mystery of the word before our souls, as it functioned and was understood when the real meaning of John's Gospel was still experienced, we must realize that spirit was present in the word for ancient human consciousness—even in the weakened words of speech. Spirit poured into the word and became its power.

I am not criticizing any period, nor am I saying that one era is less important than any other. I merely want to describe how the ages differ as they follow one another, each having its own special value. But some ages must be described in a more negative way, some more positive.

Imagine the darkness that gradually crept over the living impulse in the words of a sentence such as "In the beginning was the Word." Consider civilization of the sixteenth- or seventeenth-centuries and how humankind had to prepare for the growing inner force of freedom. One must also value elements that were absent during certain periods—in a sense, value them properly for the first time. Now consider the fact that humanity had to gain freedom in a fully conscious way, and that this would have been impossible if spirit still poured into words and inspired them as in earlier times. Then we can understand how education in its older form became impossible once Francis Bacon of Verulam made a significant statement around the seventeenth century that, when we face it honestly, implies the annihilation of the essence of a phrase such as "In the beginning was the Word." Before then, there was always a shadow of the spirit in the word, or *Logos*. Bacon asks us to see only an "idol" in the word, not spirit any longer, but an idol; one could no longer hold the word in its own power, but had to guard against the intellectualized word.

Once one loses the true essence of the word, from which knowledge, civilization, and power had been drawn in earlier times, one clings to an idol—or so believed Bacon. We see in this doctrine of idols a shift away from the word during the sixteenth and seventeenth centuries. There was a time when humankind not only received the word in word, but also in spirit—indeed, the cosmic creative spirit in the word, or *Logos*. Then came the age when the word began to mislead, as an idol does, into intellectualism. Human beings were taught to hold onto outer, sensory phenomena, lest they fall prey to the idol in the word. Bacon demanded that humankind no longer hold onto what pours into words from the gods, but hold onto the outer world and its dead objects—or, at best, objects enlivened externally. Humanity is directed away from words to the outer physical world. People are left with only the feeling that we must educate the human being, within whom the spirit is in fact present; but the word is an idol. People today can look with eyes only at what exists externally. Education no longer uses what is truly human, but what exists outside the human being.

Along with this comes the problem of education, bringing fierce enthusiasm but also today's tragedy. We see it very typically during the sixteenth and seventeenth centuries in persons of Michel de Montaigne and John Locke and (along with what was happening here in England) Amos Comenius on the Continent. In these three men— Montaigne, Locke, Comenius—we can almost see how the human departure from *Logos* and the turn toward physical objects was the strongest impulse in civilization. Fear of the idol in the word arose in humanity; *Logos* disappeared. The decisive factor was so-called observation, a justifiable function (as we shall see in following lectures) but now understood to be sensory observation. We see how anxiously Montaigne, Locke, and Comenius desired to divert humanity from the suprasensory and all that lives in the *Logos*. Locke and Comenius always pointed toward the external expressly and tried to avoid anything not available to the senses. In educating the young, they tried to bring as much of the sensory world as possible. We see Comenius writing books, whose purpose is to show that we should not work through the word, but through synthetic sensory perceptions. We see how this transition was accomplished and how humanity lost all sense of connection with spirit through the word. We understand that civilization as a whole can no longer inwardly accept something like "In the beginning was the Word," clinging instead to outer facts of senses; the *Logos* is accepted today only as tradition.

Thus a longing arises—with intense enthusiasm but also with fearful tragedy—to educate through sensory perception, because the word is considered an idol in Bacon's sense. This longing appeared most typically in Montaigne, Locke, and Comenius. But, they also show us, from their position of prominence, what lives in humanity as a whole; they show us how the mood, which is expressed today as a deep longing to return spirit to human beings, arose right when humanity could no longer believe in the spirit, but only in the idol of the word, as did Bacon. Educational reform groups, beginning with Montaigne and Comenius (and fully justified in those times), must now develop something for the sake of our time that brings spirit to human beings—spirit that has been given form and experienced and carries forces of will, something that sees spirit revealed in the human body and its earthly activities.

A new era of education begins with this rediscovery of the suprasensory within the sensory, the rediscovery of spirit that was lost to the word when word became an idol. Montaigne, Locke, and Comenius knew very well what education should be. Their programs are just as good as those of modern educational groups, and all the demands for education today were already present in the abstract writings of those three. What we need today, however, is a way that leads us to reality, because no education will develop out of abstract principles or programs, but only from reality. Because human beings are soul and spirit—because our nature is physical, soul, and spiritual—reality must return to our lives. And, along with reality, spirit will also return to our lives, and only such spirit can sustain an educational art for the future.

❖ 6 ❖

WALKING, SPEAKING, THINKING

August 10, 1923

What I have presented thus far should not simply lead to some theory about the need for a new form of education, but to a new attitude toward education. In my earlier lectures, I wanted to speak less to the intellect and more to the heart. This is most important for the teacher, because, as we've seen, we must base an art of education on a full understanding of the human being.

For some time now, whenever people discuss an art of education, we hear that it is the child who is important. There are many educational goals and, in a sense, theoretical demands about how we should approach children. But this is not the way to develop complete devotion in a teacher toward education. This is possible only when teachers can understand the whole human being, in body, soul, and spirit. Those who have living ideas about the human being (as I have described) will find that those ideas are transformed directly into volition. In a practical way, from hour to hour, teachers will learn how to answer an important question. But who asks this question? It is the children themselves. Consequently, the most important thing is to learn how to read children. And, in this, we are guided by a truly practical understanding of the human being in body, soul, and spirit.

It is difficult to speak about so-called Waldorf education, because it is not really something we can learn or
discuss. Waldorf education is strictly a practical matter,
and the only way to describe it is by using examples of
how it is practiced in one situation or another according
to specific needs. Experience determines how we practice
Waldorf education. When we begin with this attitude, we
assume that the teacher has an appropriate understanding of the human being. When this happens, in a sense
education involves very general social questions, because
teaching children should begin immediately after birth.
This means that humanity as a whole, every family and
every group of people, is responsible for education. This
is something that we understand from the nature of children before the change of teeth at the age of seven.

Jean Paul, a German writer, said something truly wonderful when he claimed that people learn more about life
during their first three years than they do in three years at
a university.[1] It is true, in fact, that the first three years as
well as the following years before seven are the most
important for the overall development of a human being.
A child is a very different being at a later age.

During those first years, a child is really an organ of
sensory perception. The problem is that people do not
usually comprehend the importance of this. We must
make very drastic statements if we are to reveal the full
truth of that idea. Later in life, when people eat, they
taste with the mouth, gums, or tongue; taste is localized
in the head. That is not true of children, especially during
the first years of life. Taste affects their entire organism.

---

1. Jean Paul (Johann Paul Friedrich Richter, 1763–1825), a novelist whose
works were popular in the early nineteenth century. His pen name
reflected his admiration for Jean-Jacques Rousseau.

Children can taste their mother's milk and their first food right down into the limbs. For a young child, what happens later only on the tongue happens throughout the entire organism. In a sense, children live by tasting everything they encounter. This is something animal-like in young children, but never imagine that this is the same as in animals. "Animal-like" in young children is, in a sense, at a higher level. A human being is never an animal, not even as an embryo—indeed, least of all at that time. We can clarify such ideas by comparing them to something else.

If you have ever observed natural processes with some understanding—say, a herd of cows grazing in a field, then lying down to digest, each devoted to the whole world in a sense—then you may have some impression of what actually occurs in an animal. An entire universe, an extract of cosmic events, is underway in an animal, and it experiences the most wonderful visions while digesting. Digestion is the most important way that animals have for understanding. While an animal digests, it devotes itself in a dreamy, imaginative way to the entire world. This might seem overstated, but the strangest thing is that it is not overstated at all and corresponds to reality. If we raise that image a step, we see the experience of a young child's physical functions. Taste accompanies all physical functions. And, just as taste accompanies all physical functions, something else permeates a child's whole organism and is later localized in the eyes and ears.

Consider the wonder of an eye. We see when it receives something formed outside and filled with color, and then creating an image inwardly. It is localized and separate from the totality of our experience. We comprehend intellectually what the eye creates in this wonderful way. The intellect makes it into a kind of shadow image. It is the same for the wonderful processes localized in an adult's ears. What is localized as a sense in adult ears, however, is spread throughout the whole organism of a young child. Thus children do not differentiate between spirit, soul, and body. Everything that affects a child from outside is re-created within. Children imitate their entire environment inwardly.

Now that we have considered matters from this perspective, let's look at how children learn three important activities during the first years: walking, speaking, and thinking. These early capacities have great importance for the rest of children's lives.

"Learning to walk" is a kind of shorthand for something much more comprehensive. Because the process of learning to walk is most obvious, we say "children learn to walk." But learning to walk is connected directly to balancing ourselves in relation to the spatial world. As children, we try to stand, trying to bring our legs into such a relationship to gravity that we gain our balance. We try to do the same with our arms and hands. Our entire body becomes oriented in this way. Learning to walk means orienting ourselves spatially.

It is important to see that young children are imitative and sensory perceptive, because, during the early years, they must learn everything through imitation, copying what happens around them. It is clear to everyone that a child's organism develops its own powers of orientation and that the human organism tends to bring itself into a vertical position and not remain horizontal, or crawling, and to bring the arms into a similar balance spatially. All of this is inherent to young children, and it arises from the organism's own impulses.

We spoil the human organism for life if, as teachers, we introduce even a little compulsion into the true desires of human nature; we should leave human nature free and act only as its assistants. If we do not simply help a child but use inappropriate external actions to force a child to begin to walk, we ruin that child's life, right up to the time of death. In particular, we ruin that child's life in old age. In properly educating a child, it is important not to look only at the present but at the child's whole life until death. We must understand that the seeds of a person's whole life exist in that individual during childhood.

Because children are very subtle organs of sensory perception, they are receptive not only to surrounding physical influences, but also to moral influences, particularly those of thoughts. As odd as this may seem to materialistic thinking today, children perceive what we think when we are around them. As parents or teachers, when we are around young children it is important not only to avoid acting in ways we should not in front of children, but we should also be inwardly true and moral in our thinking and feeling, which children can sense. Children form their being not just according to our words and actions, but also according to our attitudes, thoughts, and feelings. During this first period of childhood, before the age of seven, the most important thing for education is a child's environment.

Now we come to the problem of what we can do to guide children who are learning to walk and orient themselves. It is important that, through spiritual science, we see the living relationships that we cannot see with a dead, materialistic science. Consider a child who was forced, in all sorts of ways, to walk and find an orientation in space, simply because people felt it was the thing to do. Now imagine that child at the age of fifty or sixty. If nothing else has acted to correct the situation, we might see that this person has various metabolic illnesses, rheumatism, gout, and so on. Everything we do to children by forcing them into the vertical position so they can walk— even when we do it only halfheartedly—goes so deeply into the soul that the spirit affects the physical body. The forces we create through such dubious means remain throughout life, and, if they are not the right forces, they manifest later on as physical illnesses.

All education of young children is also physical education. You cannot isolate physical education, because all education of spirit and soul affects children's physical bodies, and thus it is also physical education. When you see children beginning to orient themselves by standing and beginning to walk, if you lovingly view the wonderful secret of the human organism that causes children to move from horizontal to vertical; if you have a feeling of reverence and modesty when you see God's creative forces in the way children orient themselves in space; if you deeply love the human nature of children, because you love every expression of human nature—in other words, when you *assist* children in learning to walk and orient themselves—you create healthy forces in children that will manifest as a healthy metabolism when they reach fifty or sixty, a time when people require some control over their metabolisms.

The true secret of human development is contained in the fact that whatever becomes ensouled and made spiritual at a certain stage of life will manifest physically later on, often after many years. This is how it works with learning to walk. A child who is guided with love into learning to walk will grow up to be healthy. Using love to help children walk makes up much of basic physical and health education.

Speech develops from a child's orientation in space. Modern physiology knows little about that, but it does know something. Physiologists recognize that, although we generally use our right hands, there is a certain area on the left side of the brain that is the source of speech. Physiology thus indicates a correspondence between movements of the right hand and the so-called Broca's Area in the left side of the brain.[2] The hand's movements, its gestures and means of strength, enters the brain and forms the source of speech. That is only a small aspect of what science knows on the subject. The fact is, however, that speech arises not only from right-hand movements (which correspond to the left side of the brain) but also from motor functions as a whole. The way children learn to walk and orient themselves spatially and the way they learn to transform their first dangling, uncontrolled movements of the arms into meaningful movements in the outer world mysteriously passes into the organization of the head. That inner organization manifests as speech.

Those who correctly understand such things also realize that children who drag their feet also vocalize, especially with the lips, in a different way than do those with a firm walk. All the nuances of speech arise from the forms of movement. Life involves gestures first; gestures are transformed inwardly into the source of speech. Speech is thus a result of walking and spatial orientation. The way a child speaks depends largely on our loving

2. Paul Pierre Broca (1824–1880), a French surgeon and anthropologist, described a patient who was able to say only one word: "tan." When the patient died, Broca examined his brain and found damage in part of the left frontal cortex, which came to be called "Broca's Area."

help when that child learns to walk. These are the subtle associations that result from a real understanding of the human being. I had a reason for going into such detail in the previous lectures about how spirit enters the human constitution. Thus, we bring the spirit to the physical body, because the physical body follows spirit with each step, as long as spirit is brought to it in the proper way.

Initially, children learn to speak by using their entire organism. When you look it, you see that first there are outer leg movements, which lead to strong contours of speech. These are followed by arm and hand movements, which lead to inflections in words and their forms. We can see that external movements lead to a flexibility of language in a child. We need to provide guidance through love when assisting children in learning to walk; likewise, when helping them in learning to speak, we need inner truth. Life's greatest lies are created while a child is learning to speak, because the truth of speech is absorbed through the physical organism.

If, as teachers, we always speak truthfully to children, they will imitate their surroundings and learn to speak so that the subtle, continuous activity of breathing will become stronger. We should not, however, think of these things in a coarse way, but very subtly. They have a very subtle existence, but they manifest throughout life. We inhale oxygen and exhale carbon dioxide. Within our bodies, we must transform oxygen into carbon dioxide through the breathing process. The world gives us oxygen and receives carbon dioxide from us. Whether we are able to transform oxygen into carbon dioxide properly depends upon whether we were treated honestly by those around us when we learned to speak. In this situation, spirit is transformed completely into the physical.

One such lie is the belief that we are doing something good by lowering our speech to childish language when we are around children. Subconsciously, children have no desire for childish language. They want to hear the real speech of adults. We should speak normally to children, not with some invented childish speech. Because of their incapacities, children initially babble imitations of what we say to them, but we should not babble. That is a big mistake. When we use babbling baby talk, we hurt a child's digestive organs, because spirit always becomes physical and affects the physical organism in its formation. Everything we do spiritually with children is also physical education, because children are insubstantial in themselves. An unhealthy digestive organ later in life is often caused by learning to speak incorrectly.

Just as speaking comes from walking and gestures, thinking develops from speaking. We need to give loving assistance when helping children learn to walk, and likewise we should pay special attention to honesty when they are learning to speak, because they inwardly imitate their surroundings. Because children are completely beings of sensory perception and physically re-create spirit, we need to emphasize clarity in our thinking, so they will develop proper thinking from speaking.

The worst thing we could do to a child is to say something and then retract it, saying something different. This leads to confusion. Using confused thinking with a child is the real cause of so-called nervousness today. Why are so many people nervous? When they were children, they learned to think after learning to speak, and the people near them did not think clearly and precisely.

The greatest mistakes in the behavior of any generation are a true reflection of the previous generation. If, later in life, you observe the children you taught and see their vices, it should make you consider yourself. There is a very close connection between everything that occurs in children's surroundings and what those children express through the physical body. In young children, the physical constitution is formed by love as they learn to walk, truthfulness as they learn to speak, and clarity and firmness in their environment as they learn to think. Children's organs and vessels form according to the way love, truthfulness, and clarity develop in their environment. Metabolic illnesses arise from learning to walk without love; digestive problems may result from untruthfulness while the child is learning to speak; and nervousness comes from confused thinking in a child's surroundings.

When you look at how common nervousness is in the 1920s, you must conclude that teachers were very confused around the beginning of the century. The confused thinking of that time manifests as nervousness today. Further, nervousness at the turn of the century is no more than a picture of the confusion around 1870. We cannot look at such things and say that there was a physiological, hygienic, and psychological education, or that a doctor should have been brought in whenever the teacher needed to handle something in a healthy way. Instead, physiological pedagogy and school hygiene form a whole, and it is part of the teacher's mission to work with the effects of spirit on the physical, sensory organism.

Because everyone is a teacher for children between birth and the age of seven, we face the social task of achieving genuine understanding of the human being. Otherwise, humanity will regress instead of moving forward. Our more humane age has rightly eliminated a common practice in schools: beating and spanking. No one should accuse me of supporting beatings, but the only reason beatings were successfully removed from our schools was because such close attention was paid to externals. Society is quite capable of seeing how physically harmful beatings are and the moral consequences arising from them. Much today is oriented toward the physical, sensory world, and little toward spirit and soul. Consequently, we have brought another form of beatings into education, a form that people do not recognize, because they look so little toward the spirit.

For example, mothers today (and to a certain extent fathers) find it very important to give "beautiful" dolls to little girls to play with. Despite the best of intentions, such dolls look horrible, because they are so inartistic. Nevertheless, people often think that a beautiful doll must have real hair, real makeup, and even moving eyes, so that the eyes close when the doll is lying down, and when you pick it up, the eyes look at you. There are even dolls that move. In other words, we give children toys that imitate life in odd, inartistic ways. Such dolls are merely typical examples. Our civilization is gradually making all toys this way. In effect, they give a terrible inner beating to children. Children may be well-behaved in public and never reveal the conventional upbringing and the beatings they receive at home; likewise, children do not reveal the antipathy deep within their souls toward so-called beautiful dolls. We force children to like them, but the unconscious forces within children, their dislike of everything about the beautiful dolls, also play a strong role. As I will show in a moment, such things beat children inwardly.

When you consider everything that children experience in their simple thinking before the age of four or five—even six or seven—while learning to stand and walk, the appropriate result will be a doll that is perhaps made from a handkerchief, with a head on top and maybe two ink spots for eyes. In this doll, you have everything a young child can understand and love. It presents the simplest characteristics of the human form—at least, to the degree that a young child can absorb it.

A child knows no more about human beings than that they stand up; they have an up and a down. And on top sits a head with a pair of eyes. In children's drawings, you often find that they draw the mouth on the forehead. The position of one's mouth is not entirely clear to young children. What a child can really experience exists in a doll made from a handkerchief with a pair of ink spots on it. An inner creative force is active within young children. Everything they receive from their environment is translated into inner development, which includes the formation of organs.

If a child's father is often angry—if at any moment, an unmotivated event could shock that child, then that is also experienced. A child experiences it in such a way that it is expressed in the breathing and circulation. Since it is expressed in the rhythmic system, it actively forms the lungs and heart—indeed, the entire circulatory system. Children carry that sculpted inner organization throughout life; it is a constitution formed by seeing the actions of an angry father.

What I said is meant only to indicate how children have a wonderful inner formative force, and how they continuously work on themselves as sculptors. If you give a child a doll made from a handkerchief, those formative forces move quietly into the brain—that is, those forces affecting the rhythmic system through breathing and blood circulation move gently into the brain and give it form. They shape a child's brain in much the same way a sculptor works with a subtle, light, spiritualized, and soulful hand. Everything proceeds through an organic development. Children look at a doll made from a handkerchief, and the formative forces arising from the rhythmic system begin to work on the brain.

If you give a child a so-called beautiful doll, one that might even be able to move or close its eyes, painted and with beautiful hair, a doll that looks so artistic but is actually quite ugly, the formative forces arising from the rhythmic system to form the brain act like the lashes of a whip. Everything a child cannot yet understand whips the brain; the brain is thoroughly beaten in a terrible way. That is the problem with "beautiful" dolls, and it is also the problem with much of children's play.

When we want to lovingly guide children's play, we must be clear about how much of their inner developmental strengths are called on. In this sense, our entire civilization sees things in the wrong way. Our society has, for example, created a form of animism. A child is hurt by bumping into a table, and then responds by striking it back. People today would say that the child has rendered the table "alive" through imagination. They say that the child "dreams" the table to life and then hits it. But this is not how it works. The child does not dream anything into the table. Rather, children dream life from real living beings. It is not that children dream life into a table; they dream life from actual living beings. When children injure themselves, they strike back out of reflex, because things are in fact without life for children. They do not dream life into a table, but respond in the same way toward animate or inanimate objects.

We can see that our civilization is unable to approach children correctly because of such backward ideas. The important thing is that we work in a truly loving way with children, so that we guide them only with love toward what they want. Consequently, we should not beat children inwardly with "beautiful" dolls. We should live with them and make a doll that reflects the way they experience it inwardly.

And this is true of all play. Play requires real understanding of childhood. If we babble like a small child, if we reduce our language to that of a child and do not speak as they should hear and as is appropriate to our own nature, we present children with a lie. We should not, however, place ourselves in a position of untruthful speech, but we should place ourselves specifically at the level of children in relation to willed activities, specifically play. If we do that, it will be clear that intellectuality, which our civilization loves so much, exists nowhere in children. Thus, we should not interject anything influenced by intellect into children's play.

Children naturally imitate in their play what occurs in their surroundings. We seldom see children who want to be, say, linguists when they play. It would certainly be a rare experience for a four-year-old to have ambitions to be a linguist. Under some circumstances, however, a child might want to be a chauffeur. Why? Because we can see everything a chauffeur does, and it makes a direct pictorial impression. But there is no image of what a linguist does, and it completely passes by a child's life. We should involve only those things that do not go unnoticed by children, and intellectual things pass them by. What do we, as adults, need to guide children's play properly? Adults plow fields, make hats, sew clothing, and so on. All of this is oriented toward the practical, and within it lies the intellectual. Wherever we find a goal in life, we have penetrated it with the intellect.

On the other hand, everything in life, besides being directed toward a goal, also has an outer form—whether plowing or something like building a wagon or shoeing horses. When you see a farmer guiding a plow through the furrows, aside from the goal of the activity, we feel (if I may use the expression) what lives in that image. If, as adults, we can work our way through to understand what exists in an activity aside from its purpose, we can present it to children in play. Our sense of aesthetics enables us to do that. In particular, by not pursuing the kind of beauty that today's dolls strive for, which is completely intellectual, but by going into what speaks to human feeling, we arrive at that primitive, genuinely enjoyable doll that looks more like this [a doll carved by a Waldorf student], not the so-called beautiful doll. But this, of course, is something for older children.

Most important, educators should be able to see the aesthetics of work in the activity itself, so that we can present this as we make toys. If we bring such aesthetics into the toys we make, we approach what children really want. We have become almost completely utilitarian, or intellectual, in our civilization, and thus we present children with all kinds of invented things. It is important, however, not to present young children with things from later life, things we think up. Instead, we want to give them something they can *feel* when they become older. This is what needs to be in toys. We may want to give a boy a toy plow, but it is important that we instill into that toy something formative and aesthetic about plowing. This fully develops the strength of human beings.

This is where many otherwise good kindergartens make major mistakes. The Fröbel kindergarten and others created with a genuine love of children must become clear that young children are imitative, but they can imitate only what is not intellectual. Therefore, we should not bring all kinds of invented activities into a kindergarten. Games such as pick-up sticks or braiding, which often play such an important role in kindergarten, are simply invented. In kindergarten, we should do only the things that big people do, not things invented for play. People who really understand human nature are often overcome by a tragic feeling when they come into these well-intended kindergartens. On the one hand, there is an endless amount of goodwill there and much love for the children. On the other hand, there is no consideration for the fact that everything is intellectual. Kindergartens should exclude everything that is thought up for children's play, and kindergarten children should imitate only visible adult activities.

When we train children intellectually before the age of four or five, they take something terrible into life: materialism. The more we raise children intellectually at such an early age, the more we create materialists for later life. The brain develops in such a way that spirit lives within its form, but people intuit inwardly that everything is merely physical, because the brain was taken over by intellectualism at an early age.

If you want to educate people to understand spirit, you must wait as long as possible to present the intellectual version of the externally spiritual. Although it is necessary, especially today, for people to be completely awake in later life, it is equally necessary to let children live in their gentle dreamy experiences as long as possible, so that they move slowly into life. They need to remain as long as possible in their imaginations and pictorial capacities without intellectuality. In our modern civilization, if you allow the organism to be strengthened without intellectualism, children will move into the necessary intellectualism in the proper way.

If you beat a child's brain as I described, you will ruin the soul for the rest of life. Just as you ruin a person's digestion by babbling, or a person's metabolism by a lack of love, likewise you ruin a person's soul by beating a child from within. An ideal of our education must be to avoid beating a child's soul, and because a child is united as a being of body, soul, and spirit, we must also eliminate the inner physical beatings. In other words, our ideal is to eliminate so-called beautiful dolls and, most important, to bring play to the proper level.

I would like to conclude my remarks today by saying again that we need to avoid what is falsely spiritual, so that what is properly spiritual—the whole human being—can appear later in life.

7

RHYTHM, SLEEP, IMITATION

August 11. 1923

The transition from early childhood to school is marked by the change of teeth around the seventh year, and in studying this period it must be remembered that, until the seventh year, children work, so to speak, as inner sculptors. Formative forces emanate from the head, organizing and shaping the child's whole being. Everything in a child's environment, including the moral qualities, now plays a role in developing the vascular system, the circulation of the blood, and the processes of breathing, so that, as physical beings, we bear within us throughout life the results of the imitative period of childhood, from birth until the second dentition.

It cannot be said, of course, that this is our only conditioning, because much can be rectified in the body later through the exercise of moral forces and inner soul activity. Nevertheless, we should recognize what a wonderful heritage we can give children on their path through life if we help make their physical body into a container for moral, spiritual qualities. If, in other words, we help children's inner sculptor up to the age of seven by bringing them only what is moral and conducive to fruitful activity in life. I spoke more in detail about these things yesterday, and much more will emerge as the lectures proceed.

Teachers, therefore, must understand that once children have passed their seventh year, these formative forces are transformed into soul activity, so that they long for imagery, and this should indicate the fundamental principle of childhood education.

After the second dentition until adolescence, most important is the development of the rhythmic system—the breathing and blood circulation, along with everything related to the rhythm of digestive functions. Whereas teachers find a need for imagery in children's souls, they have to work with the rhythmic system as an organic system. Consequently, an imaginative element must prevail in all the child's tasks. I would say that a musical quality must pervade the relationship between teachers and students. Rhythm, measure, and even melody must be present as the basic principle of teaching, and thus teachers must have this musical quality within themselves and in their lives as a whole. The rhythmic system dominates in children's organic nature during this first period of school, and their education must follow a certain rhythm. Teachers must possess this musical element so deeply—in a sense instinctively—that true rhythm will prevail in the classroom.

It is evident that, during the early years of school (after the age of seven), real education must arise from a foundation of art. The reason why education today leaves so much to be desired is that modern civilization is not conducive to the development of an artistic feeling. I am not referring to any particular art, but to the fact that sound educational principles can develop only from an entirely artistic view of civilization. This is very significant.

If we can imbue our teaching with an artistic quality, we influence children's rhythmic systems. Such teaching makes a child's breathing and circulation healthier. We must be clear that, on the one hand, our task is to lead children into life, to help them develop a sound faculty of judgment for later life, and so at this age we must teach them to use their intelligence, but not through any form of coercion. On the other hand, we must help children toward health in later life, insofar as their destiny permits. Thus, we must pay enough attention to physical care and exercise. To accomplish this, however, we need a deeper understanding of the whole human being.

In our culture, in which all eyes are focused on material things, no attention is directed to the condition of sleep, even though we devote one-third of our earthly lives to it. This rhythm of waking and sleeping is extremely important. We should never think that we are not active when we sleep. We are inactive only in relation to the outer world, but in terms of the body's health, and more important, the health of the soul and spirit, sleep is very important. Real education can provide for a proper life of sleep, because whatever we do during our waking hours, it is carried into sleep, and this is especially true of children.

We must understand only this: the rhythmic system, the basis of all artistic activity, never becomes tired. Breathing and the heart activity continue from birth to death. It is only the processes of thought and volition that lead to fatigue. Thinking and physical movement cause fatigue, and because they are always involved, we can say that all life's activities lead to fatigue. In the case of children, however, we must be especially careful that this happens as little as possible. We can do this by making sure that during the early school years, our teaching has an essential quality of art, because we then call on the rhythmic system of children, which tires least of all.

What happens, then, if we demand too much of the intellect by urging children to think? It involves certain organic forces that tend to harden the body inwardly. Such forces lead to saline deposits in the body and form bone, cartilage, and tendons—all those parts of the body that tend to become rigid. Normal rigidity becomes over-developed if intellectual thinking is forced. We are at work inwardly on hardening our organism while we are awake, and if we require too much of the intellect, too much hardening takes place. When we force children to think too much, it can lead to premature hardening of the arteries.

Consequently, it is essential to truly observe the nature of a child and develop a fine sense of just how much we should demand, because a vital principle is at stake. If we ask children to think by teaching them to learn letters and write in an intellectual way, we stress their mental powers and sow the seeds of a tendency toward sclerosis. Human beings have absolutely no inner relationship to the letters of modern writing. They are little "demons" insofar as human nature is concerned, and we must find the right way to approach them. We find this way by first engaging children's artistic feeling, letting them paint or draw the lines and colors that flow on their own onto the paper from their innermost being. Then, when a child is artistically active in this way, one always feels—and feeling is the essential thing—that people are too enriched by the artistic activity. One gets the sense that intellectuality impoverishes the soul and makes us inwardly barren, whereas artistic activity makes us inwardly rich—too rich, in fact, so that it must be modified in some way. Artistic imagery tends to pass automatically into a more attenuated form of concepts and ideas, and it becomes necessary to impoverish the artistic aspect by intellectual-izing it. After stimulating a child artistically, however, if we then allow intellectuality to develop from that artistic feeling, the artistic element will have the right intensity. It will take hold of the body so that a balanced hardening can take place.

By forcing the intellectual powers of children, we hinder their growth; we liberate those forces, however, by approaching the intellect through art. Thus, during the early school years, a Waldorf school tries to educate through art rather than through the intellect. Teaching thus begins with imagery, not intellect. The teacher-child relationship is pervaded by music and rhythm, and thus we attain the necessary degree of intellectual develop-ment in children. Consequently, mental training is also the very best physical education.

To a more sensitive observer, there is plenty of evi-dence today that many adults are too rigid inwardly. They seem to drag their bodies around like wooden machines. It is really typical of our time that people carry their bodies as though they were burdens, whereas a more genuine and artistic education develops people, so that every step and gesture, which will later benefit humanity, provides an inner sense of joy and well-being. By educating intellectually, we loosen the soul from the body, and one goes through life feeling that the body is merely "of the earth," so that it has no value and must be overcome. As a result, we may give ourselves to a purely mystical life of soul and spirit, feeling that only spirit has value. When we educate correctly, however, it leads us through truth to spirit, the creative spirit within the body. God did not create the world with the notion that matter is evil and must be avoided. No world would have come into being if that had been the gods' thought. The world emanated from divine spirit only because the gods ordained that spirit would be directly and immediately active in matter.

Once people realize that their best path in every area of life is directed by divine intention, they will choose an education that does not alienate them from the world, but transforms them into beings whose soul and spirit remain with the body throughout life. Anyone who must continually cast off the body to become immersed in thought is no real thinker.

The waking life is related to everything we are able to do in a healthy way to develop the intellect on the basis of artistic activity; all physical culture, however, has a definite relationship to a child's sleep. To understand what constitutes a healthy physical education, we must first understand how physical exercise affects a child's sleep. All physical activity that arises from the will through the soul is indeed a flow of volitional impulses into the motor system. Even in purely mental activity, the will is active and flowing into the limbs. If you sit at a desk and decide what tasks others will do, volitional impulses also flow into your limbs. In this case, we merely hold them back. You may sit still, but the orders you give are, in fact, an influx of volition into your limbs. Consequently, you must discover what is important in those physically active will impulses before their development can affect sleep in the right way.

Everything transformed into action by the human will causes a process of organic combustion. When I think, I solidify my organism and deposit solids in it. With my will, I burn up something in my organism—but this inner process of combustion must not be thought of as physical combustion, like that of chemistry or physics. When a candle is lit, an external process of combustion occurs, but only materialistic thinking would compare the process of inner combustion to the flame of a candle. In the human organism, the soul and spirit take hold of the processes of outer nature so that within the human body, and even in a plant, the outer substances of nature are active in a very different way. Likewise, the burning process in a human being is completely different from the process of combustion in a candle. Nevertheless, a certain kind of combustion is always induced in the body when we will, even when the impulse does not cause us to move physically. Because we generate inner combustion, we do something to our organism that only sleep can rectify. In a sense, our bodies would literally burn up if sleep did not reduce combustion to the proper intensity—not in the crude sense of natural science, but in a subtle, more intimate way. Sleep regulates inner combustion by spreading it throughout the organism; otherwise, it would remain confined to the organs of movement.

There are two ways to accomplish physical movement. Consider the exercises children are often asked to do. The idea is (everything is "idea" in a materialistic age, despite the belief that one is dealing with facts) that children should move in certain ways in games or gymnastic exercises, because this is how they grow up to be civilized human beings. As a rule, the best movements are those that adults are used to, because the goal is that children should grow up to be exact replicas of their elders. Thus, they are required to do the same sort of gymnastics. In other words, there will be a certain opinion about what is appropriate to the right sort of adult, and this is, in turn, applied to the child.

Thus, out of an abstract idea, although it involves the actual, one forces something material on children. Gymnastic apparatus is so contrived that it requires children to make the desired specific movements. But this initiates combustion processes that the human organism can no longer regulate. As a result, such methods of physical education lead to restless sleep. Again, such matters are not so physically obvious that they can be confirmed by conventional medicine, but they occur nevertheless in the finer, more subtle processes of the human body. When we give children such conventional gymnastic exercises, they cannot get the deep, sound sleep they need, and the physical constitution is not sufficiently restored by sleep.

When we educate children by bringing everything to them in an artistic way, then just as an overly rich artistic life leads to a longing for the impoverishing nature of intellectual work (the intellect is drawn in an elemental way out of the artistic), similarly a hunger for physical activity arises in children who are engaged artistically. This occurs because artistic work involves the whole being. Nothing produces a craving for physical exercise the way artistic activity does. When children have been occupied artistically for perhaps two hours (and the time must be carefully regulated), something that longs for expression as specific body movements begins to stir in the organism. Art creates a real hunger for the right movements of the body.

Thus, after children have been busy painting and drawing with their hands, singing with their voices, or playing musical instruments (and this should begin as soon as possible), we gradually lead those activities into the spatial movement of play. We must continue that inner artistic activity of the children. Physical education is drawn from the other efforts at school, and there is an intimate connection between the two.

If children are given no more physical exercise than they desire because of their artistic work, they will get the kind of sleep they need. We can help children live right while awake by drawing the intellectual out of the artistic, and, as a result, we also cultivate the right sleep, in which all the organic processes of combustion are harmonized. For the body, nothing is more important than thoroughly artistic teachers. The more joy a teacher can experience in beautiful forms, in music, the more that teacher longs to move from abstractions toward rhythm and poetry; the more musical formation there is in a teacher, the better that teacher will be able to arrange games and exercises that offer children the opportunity for artistic expression. Unfortunately, however, today's civilization would like easy access to spirit, and people are disinclined to work very hard for spiritual ideals.

As I have said before, while admitting the inadequacy of their own education, people claim to know how education should be reformed, and they are ready to make laws to support their views. There is no real inclination to consider the subtle processes of the human organism. People do not ask how gymnastics can arise from artistic activity or what the human organism longs for as spatial movement. And little artistic sensibility is applied to solve these problems. The main occupation of modern intellectuals is to read books; they study Greek ideals, and the latest fad becomes a revival of the "Olympic Games," although it is purely external. The Olympic Games are never studied from the perspective of what the human organism needs, as the Greeks did, because modern study always involves books or traditions that have been handed down.

Modern people are not, of course, ancient Greeks and do not understand the role of the Olympic Games in Greek culture. In those days, children were taught dancing, wrestling, and such by gymnasts, as I described. But where did the Greeks learn this? They learned it from the Olympic Games, which were not just artistic, but also religious—a true offspring of Greek culture. In the Olympic Games, the Greeks gave themselves up completely to an atmosphere of art and religion, and, thus, with a true educational instinct, they could bring these elements into the gymnastic exercises they gave to children.

Abstract, prosaic, inartistic forms of physical culture are contrary to all real education, because they are contrary to true human development. Instead of looking in books to find out how to revive the Olympic Games, it would be far better if people tried to understand inner human nature. They would discover that, unless physical education is based on inner needs, it causes too much combustion. The result of such exercises for children is a flabby muscular system later on in life. The muscles lose their ability to follow the soul and spirit.

The body becomes hardened inwardly when we educate incorrectly through the intellect for waking life. It causes people to carry their bones as though the skeleton were in fact a burden, rather than moving flexibly with the soul. Added to this are flaccid limbs, overly inclined to combustion. A person gradually becomes like a balloon attached to a log, weighed down by the salts of the body. Yet, because of inappropriate inner combustion processes, a person wants to escape from it. An intimate knowledge of the human being is needed to establish the correct relationship between the two processes of combustion and salt formation.

We can balance the hardening caused by leading artistic activities into the intellectual if we encourage the kind of combustion that brings deep and peaceful sleep to children. Thus, we eliminate the restlessness caused by most modern systems of physical education. Children who are forced to practice inappropriate physical exercises fidget inwardly during sleep, and in the morning, when the soul returns to the body, restlessness and faulty inner combustion are the result.

Thus, we must expand our concepts with knowledge, because all of this shows that it is essential to have a deep understanding of human nature. If we consider humanity to be the gods' most precious creation in our earthly existence, we must certainly ask what it is that the gods have presented to us as the human being. What is the best way we can develop the human beings entrusted to us? Until the seventh year, children are thoroughly imitative, and after the change of teeth, a child's inner nature tries to form itself according to what natural authority—in the broadest sense—reveals to it.

Quite some time ago, I wrote *Intuitive Thinking As Spiritual Activity*.[1] In view of what I said there, I do not think you will accuse me of unduly emphasizing any particular social principle. Although what human life reveals is spiritually free, it is equally subject to the laws of nature. It is, therefore, not for us to decide, according to our likes or dislikes, what sort of education we should give our children between the time of the change of teeth and adolescence. Education should be dictated by the needs of human nature itself. Accordingly, up to the second dentition, at about seven, in every gesture and attitude, even in

---

1. *Die Philosophie der Freiheit* (1895), originally published in English as *The Philosophy of Spiritual Activity.*

the blood's pulse, in rhythm of breath, and in the various vessels, children imitate everything that happens around them. From birth until the age of seven, the environment is the model that children copy. Similarly, from seven to puberty, children must develop free spiritual activity under the influence of natural authority. This must happen for healthy and free development, and for the proper use of freedom in later life. The faculty of individual judgment does not develop fully until fourteen or fifteen. By then, children have developed enough so that teachers are justified in appealing to their judgment. At fourteen or fifteen, children can reason for themselves, but before then we harm them and retard their development by continually discussing "why" and "how" with them.

All of later life benefits immeasurably if, between approximately seven and fourteen, children were able to accept a fact because simply because a revered teacher considered it true—not because they saw an underlying reason; indeed, their intellect was not mature enough for that. Children's sense of beauty develops properly if they are able to accept the standard of a teacher whom they spontaneously and freely respect. Children experience goodness and follow its path in later life if, instead of giving them a code of behavior to follow, we help them realize, through our own heartfelt words, how much we love benevolent actions and hate bad ones. The teacher's words can make children warmly responsive to goodness and coldly averse to evil, so that they naturally turn to the goodness, because their teacher loves it.

Children thus grow up, not bound up in dogma, but filled with spontaneous love for truth, beauty, and goodness according to a beloved teacher. During the first period of school, if children have learned to adopt the

teacher's standard of truth, beauty, and goodness—
which they have been able to express as artistic imagery—these virtues become second nature, because it was
not the intellect that developed those qualities. Those
who have been told repeatedly and dogmatically what to
do or not do develop a cold, apathetic feeling for goodness. But those who learned in childhood to feel sympathy for goodness and antipathy toward evil—who
through feeling preserved an enthusiasm for goodness
and the power to avoid evil—absorbed, right into the
rhythmic organism, a capacity to respond to goodness
and feel aversion to evil. Later on in life, it is as though,
under the influence of evil, they could hardly breathe, as
if the breathing and rhythmic systems were adversely
affected by evil.

This is, in fact, possible to achieve if, after a child has
reached the seventh year, we allow the principle of natural authority to supersede that of imitation, which must
predominate in the earlier years, as we have seen. Of
course, authority must not be enforced; this is exactly the
mistake made by those teaching methods that try to
enforce authority by using corporal punishment.

I heard that what I said about this yesterday seemed to
suggest that this type of punishment has already been
superseded. In fact, what I really said was that today's
humanitarian feelings would like to eliminate it. I was
told that the custom of whipping students in England is
still common, and that I created the wrong impression. I
am sorry that my words were taken this way, but the
point I want to make is that, in true education, authority
must never be maintained by force, and above all not by
using a whip. Authority must arise naturally from what
we are. In body, soul, and spirit, we become true teachers

once our observation of human nature brings us true understanding of humanity. Genuine observation sees a work of divine creation in a growing human being. There is no more wonderful sight in the world than to see a child, from birth on, gradually develop in body toward the definite from the indefinite—to see irrelevant, arbitrary movements transformed into movements determined by the soul, to see the inner being begin to express itself externally, as the spiritual element in the body gradually surfaces. The being that the divine world sent to earth and that we see revealed in the body becomes a revelation of the divine itself.

A growing human being is indeed divine spirit's most splendid manifestation. If we come to understand a growing human being—not through ordinary anatomy and physiology, but by understanding how soul and spirit stream into the body—then all our knowledge of humanity becomes real humility and reverence in face of what flows to the surface of things from divine depths. As teachers, this gives us a certain quality that sustains us, and for children it becomes a natural authority that they trust spontaneously. Instead of arming ourselves with a whip or some form of inner punishment, which I mentioned yesterday, we should arm ourselves with a deep knowledge of the human being and a capacity for real observation. This becomes an inner sense of morality and reverence for God's creation. With this, we gain a true position in the school, and we realize how absolutely essential it is that all educators watch for the moments when a child's whole nature experiences a complete transformation.

A change like this occurs, for example, between nine and ten, although one child may be earlier, another later.

Much in life passes unnoticed by a materialist, but true observation of the human being tells us that something remarkable happens between nine and ten. Externally, children become restless; they cannot deal with the outer world and seem to timidly withdraw. In a subtle way, this happens to almost all children—in fact, it is normal. We must see this, because in children's feelings, an important question arises at this time, but they cannot form the question mentally or express it in words. It is all a matter of feeling; thus it is even stronger and calls all the more intensely for recognition. What do children look for at this age?

Up to this age, reverence for their teachers has been a natural inner impulse. Now, however, they want their teachers to prove worthy of reverence in some way. Uncertainty arises, and when we see this we must respond. There is no need to think about it; we may be especially loving and encouraging with them. Whatever we do, we save them from a precipice because of our particular attitude, and because children see that we enter their situation with their best interests at heart. This has far-reaching significance, because if they remain insecure, it will continue throughout life, unnoticed by them, but expressed in personality, temperament, and physical health.

We must understand how spirit affects all matter and, thus, physical health, and how spirit must be nurtured so it can affect health in the right way. A genuine art of education emphatically demonstrates the need to harmonize spirit and matter. We must recognize what we owe to the education of modern civilization. It has separated everything, and when we think about nature we do so within today's materialism. When people become dissatisfied with the results of this view of nature, they invent spiritualism, which tries to reach spirit in a way that contradicts science. This is one of the tragedies of our day. Materialism has intellectualized everything and comprehends only its own views, so it can never reach the heart of matter. And modern spiritualism? Its followers want tangible spirits, who manifest physically through table tapping and other such phenomena. Spirits must not remain spiritual, invisible, and intangible, because people are too lazy to penetrate to where spirit really exists.

Humankind has fallen into a strange and tragic situation. Materialism speaks exclusively of matter, never spirit. But in reality, materialism cannot even understand matter and describes it only in distilled abstractions, whereas spiritualism, thinking it speaks of spirit, is also concerned exclusively with matter. Today's civilization is thus divided into materialists and spiritualists—a strange phenomenon indeed. Materialism cannot understand matter, and spiritualism cannot understand spirit.

Thus we are left with the remarkable fact that human wholeness has fallen into a division of body and spirit. True education must harmonize the two. It cannot be too strongly emphasized that the goal of education must be to help humankind regain its understanding of spirit in matter; it must grasp the material world through spirit. We find spirit by understanding how to take hold of the material world in the right way, and if we understand something of spirit, instead of materialized spirituality, we find a true and real spiritual world.

To educate humanity properly, moving upward, not downward, we need the reality of the spirit world and an intelligent understanding of the material world.

8

READING, WRITING, NATURE STUDY

August 13, 1923

In the previous lectures I showed that when children reach the usual age for school (at the transitional change of teeth), all teaching should be given artistically in the form of images. Today, I will take those ideas further and show how this method appeals directly to a child's heart and feelings and how everything develops from this.

A few examples will show how writing can arise from the artistic element of painting and drawing. I have already said that, if education is to be in harmony with natural human development, children must be taught to write before they learn to read. This is because one's whole being is more active in writing than it is when reading. Writing involves the movement of only one member of the body, but the forces of one's whole being become involved in this movement. When reading, only the head and the intellect are engaged, and in a truly organic form of education, everything must be developed from the qualities and forces of a child's whole nature.

We will assume that we have been able to give our students some idea of flowing water; they have learned to imagine waves and flowing water. Now we can direct their attention to the initial sound, the initial letter, of the

word *wave*. We turn our attention to the initial letter of descriptive words as we speak them. We show that the water's surface, as it rises into waves, follows this line.

After making the movement of this line, we ask the children to draw it, thus making a *w*. Thus we introduce the form of the letter *w* in writing. The *w* arose from the picture of a wave.

First, children are given mental images that can lead to letters, which they then learn to write. We might have them draw a mouth, for example. Then we introduce them to the first letter of the word *mouth*. Next, they

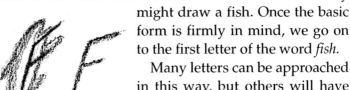

might draw a fish. Once the basic form is firmly in mind, we go on to the first letter of the word *fish*.

Many letters can be approached in this way, but others will have to be derived somewhat differently. For example, suppose we give the children an imaginative idea of the movement and sound of wind. This is the best way for little children, though there are, of course, many possibilities. We describe the rushing wind and let the children imitate its sound and arrive at a form like this:

We can develop most of the consonants by painting the forms of objects, movements, or activities.

In the case of the vowels, we must turn instead to gestures, because vowels express our inner being. The letter *a* ("ah") contains a sense of wonder and astonishment. Eurythmy is a great help here, because it gives us the gestures that truly correspond to feelings. The sounds of the letters *i*, *a*, and other vowels can be drawn from their corresponding gestures in eurythmy, since vowels should be derived from the movements that accompany the feeling life of human beings.

In this way, we can move into the abstract nature of writing from the concrete elements of painting and drawing. We then lead children to begin with the feelings evoked by an image; they thus gain the ability to relate the letters themselves to the soul quality in the feeling. The underlying principle of writing thus arises from the feeling life of the soul.

When it comes to reading, we must simply try to get children to recognize—in their heads, now—what was already elaborated through their physical forces as a whole. Reading is thus seen as an activity in which the children have already been involved. This is extremely significant. The whole process of development is ruined if children are led immediately into abstraction—if we teach them to do something by giving them purely mental concepts. Healthy growth, on the other hand, is always the result of introducing an activity first, followed by the idea, which develops from the activity. Reading is essentially mental, and if it is taught before writing, children prematurely develop only the head instead of the forces of their whole being.

Methods such as these can guide education into an area that embraces the whole human being: the realm of art. This must, in fact, be the goal of all teaching up to the age of about nine and a half. Image, rhythm, measure—these qualities must imbue all our teaching. Everything else is premature.

Consequently, before this time it was impossible to convey anything to children that strongly distinguishes between them and the outer world. It is not until around the ninth or tenth year that children begin to realize they are beings apart from the outer world. Hence, when they first come to school, we must make all outer things seem alive. We speak about the plants as living beings, conversing with us and one another in such a way that the children's view of nature and people is full of imagination. Plants, trees, and clouds all speak to children, and at this young age they must not feel separate from the outer world. In an artistic way, we must give children the feeling that just as they can speak, everything that surrounds them also speaks.

During these early years, the more we respond to the needs of children's innermost being, the more we enable them to flow into their environment. We vividly describe plants, animals, and stones so that articulate spirituality wafts toward them in weaving imaginations. These are the years when the feeling of children's souls must flow into their breathing, blood circulation, and into the whole vascular system—indeed, into the whole human organism. If we teach in this way, children's feelings will be called on in a way that is appropriate for today. Thus, children develop naturally in body and soul. It benefits children immensely when we develop this element of feeling in writing and then allow a faint echo of the intellect to enter as they rediscover in reading what they already experienced in writing. There is then a gentle accompaniment from the intellect. This is the best way to lead children toward their ninth year.

Between approximately seven and ten, it is essential for teachers to appeal directly to feeling. Children must receive the various letters into their feelings. This is very important. We unduly harden children's nature—overstrengthen the forces of bones, cartilage, and tendons in relation to the rest of the organism—when we teach them to write mechanically, asking them to trace arbitrary curves and lines for the letters, using only the physical mechanism without calling on the eye as well. If we call on the eye (which is of course connected with the movements of the hand), it will take pleasure in the results of its activity by developing the letters in an artistic way. Thus, letters do not arise merely from mechanical movements of the hand. Qualities of the soul are brought into play, and the feeling life develops at an age when it flows best into the physical body with healing power.

What you would say if you saw someone sitting with a plate of fish, carefully cutting away the flesh and eating the bones? You would probably be afraid that the person would choke and, in any case, be unable to digest the bones. On another level—that of the soul—this is exactly what happens if we give children dry, abstract ideas instead of living pictures that engage their whole being. Dry, abstract concepts must be used only to support the images that arise in the soul. When we use an imaginative, pictorial method in teaching, as I have described, we orient children's nature so that their concepts will always be flexible. We find that, once children reach the age of nine or nine and a half, we can lead them in a beautifully organic way to understand a world where they need to learn how to distinguish between themselves and their environment.

If we have devoted enough time to speaking of plants that speak to us, allowing children to look at the plant world and experience it in living pictures, we can introduce something else. They learn this in the best possible way from plants, if we begin to speak of it between the children's ninth and tenth years and gradually carry it further during the tenth and eleventh years. At this age, the human organism is ready to inwardly relate to the plant world through ideas. But, in an education whose goal is the living development of the human being, the way we speak of the plants must be very different from methods that are used simply because they were used in our own education.

It is absolutely meaningless for human life (unless, of course, it's merely a conventional one) to give children plants or flowers just so they can learn the names or the number of stamens and petals. Anything taught to children in this way remains foreign to them. They know only that they are being forced to learn it, and those who teach botany in this way to children of ten or eleven know nothing about the real connections of nature.

If we study a plant by itself, preserve it in a herbarium, and then lay it out on a table for study, it is no different than pulling out a hair and observing it. A single hair is nothing; it cannot grow on its own and has no meaning apart from the human head. Its only meaning is simply the fact that it grew on someone's head or on some animal's skin. Real meaning is found only in connections. Similarly, a plant has living significance only in its relationship to the earth, to the sun's forces, and to other forces I will speak of now. Thus, when teaching children about a plant, we must consider it only in its relationship to earth and sun.

I can sketch only roughly something that you can illustrate through pictures in many of your lessons. Here is the earth (see drawing); the roots of the plant are intimately connected to the earth. As for plants, the only thought we should awaken in children is that earth and root belong together, and their only thought about blossoms should be that they are drawn from the plant by sunlight. Children are thus led out into the cosmos in a living way.

Teachers who have enough inner vitality can tell children at this age about how a plant is placed with life in cosmic existence. First, we awaken a feeling of how the substances of earth permeate the root, which struggles to free itself from the earth by sending a shoot upward. The shoot is born from the earth and develops into leaf and flower through the light and warmth of the sun. The sun draws out the blossoms, and the earth retains the root. Then we point out—again in a living way—that the moist earth, having a watery nature, works very differently on the root than does dry earth; roots shrivel in dry soil, and come to life and fill with sap in watery earth.

Again, we explain how the sun's rays, falling straight down on the earth, call forth the flowers of plants such as yellow dandelions, buttercups, and roses. But when sunlight falls at a sharper angle, as if stroking the plant, we have plants such as the mauve autumn crocus and so on. Everywhere, we can point to living connections between roots and earth and between blossoms and sun. Having thus placed the children's imagination into the cosmos in a lively way, we describe how its growth as a whole is eventually concentrated in the seeds, from which new plants will grow.

Then, one day, to anticipate the future in a way suited to the children, we begin to reveal a truth that is still difficult to speak about openly, because conventional science considers it pure superstition or mystical fantasy. Nevertheless it is a fact that, just as the sun draws the colored blossom out of plant, the moon's forces develop and bring forth the contracting seeds. Thus, we place the plant as a living phenomenon into the activities of sun, moon, and earth. True, we cannot yet go into the function of those moon forces, because if children were to go home and speak about a connection between seeds and moon forces, scientifically minded friends might prevail upon parents to remove their children from such a school, even if they themselves were willing to accept such ideas. In these materialistic times, we have to be a bit reticent on this and many other subjects. I used this extreme example to show you the necessity of developing living ideas drawn from reality, and not from things that have no existence in themselves, because, in itself a plant has no existence without the sun and the earth.

We must now show the children something else. Here is the earth; it bulges out a bit and makes a hill, and the hill is penetrated by the forces of air and sun. It is no longer only earth substance, but changes into something between a sappy leaf and a root in the dry earth—a tree trunk. This plant has grown out of the earth, and branches also grow. The child realizes that the tree trunk is really the earth, which has sprouted upward. This also gives an idea of the inner relationship between the earth and whatever eventually acquires a woody quality. To bring this home to the children, we show how the wood decays, becoming increasingly earthly, until it finally becomes dust, and thus like the earth itself. Then we explain how sand and stone began with what was once destined to become plant, how the earth is like one huge plant or giant tree, out of which the various plants grow like branches.

Now we develop an idea that children can understand—that the earth itself is a living being, with plants as an integral part of it. It is very important that children are not given the distorted ideas of modern geology— that the earth consists only of mineral substances and forces. The formative forces of plants are as much a part of the earth as are the mineral forces. So, another point of great significance: we avoid speaking about minerals as such. Children are curious about many things, but we find that they are no longer anxious to know what stones are if we give them a living idea of plants as an integral part of the earth, drawn forth from the earth by the sun. Children really have no interest in minerals as such. And it is very beneficial if, up to the eleventh or twelfth year, they are uninterested in dead mineral substances, and instead think of the earth as a living being, like a tree that has already crumbled to dust, and from which all the plants grow like so many branches.

From this perspective, it is easy to advance to the various plants. For example, I tell the children that the roots of a certain plant are trying to find soil; its blossoms, remember, are drawn out by the sun. Suppose the roots do not find any soil, but only decaying earth. The result will be that the sun does not trouble itself to draw out the blossoms. Thus, we have a plant that fails to find the earth properly. It has no real roots and no real flower— like a fungus or mushroom. We explain how a plant like a fungus, having found no proper soil in the earth, is able to take root where the earth has already become somewhat plantlike, in the plant hill of the tree's trunk. And gray-green lichen, a parasitic plant, appears on the tree. In this way, we can draw something from the living earth forces that expresses itself in the various plants. When children have been given living ideas of plant growth, we can move on to survey the earth's face.

Yellow flowers abound in certain regions; in others, plants are stunted in their growth, and in each case the earth's face is different. Now we come to geography, which, if we lead up to it with plants, can play a very important role in children's development. We should try to give children an idea of the earth's face by relating the forces active on its surface to the varied plant life in the various regions. Then we develop a living intellect in children, not a dead one. The best age for this is between the ages of nine and twelve. We should give children a view of the interweaving activity on earth, whose inner life force produces the myriad forms of plants. Thus, we give them living ideas.

Ideas must develop, just as a limb does on one's body. A limb must develop in earliest youth. If we were to enclose a hand within an iron glove, it could not grow. Yet it is constantly said that the ideas we give children should be the most definite possible—they should define—and children should always be forming these. But nothing is more harmful to a child than definitions and sharply contoured ideas, because they lack the quality of growth. Human beings must grow as their organism grows. And child must be given flexible concepts—ideas whose form constantly changes as they mature. If we have a certain idea at the age of forty, it should not merely duplicate something we learned at the age of ten. It should have changed form, just as one's limbs and organism as a whole have changed.

We cannot stimulate living ideas in children by giving them so-called science—dead knowledge that frequently teaches us nothing at all. Rather, we give children ideas of what lives in nature. Then their souls develop in a body that grows as nature itself. We do not then go the usual route of education, which plants in children—who are engaged in a process of natural development—elements of soul life that are dead and unable to grow. We foster living, growing souls in living, growing physical organisms, and this alone serves as true development. We can stimulate real development through a study of plants and their intimate connection with the earth. Children should feel the life of the earth and plant as a unity; knowledge of the earth should be knowledge of the plant world. First, they should be shown how minerals are a residue of life, for a tree decays and becomes dust. At the particular age I am speaking of, we should teach nothing about minerals. Children must first receive concepts about what is alive; this is essential.

Just as the world of plants should be related to the earth, and children should learn to think of them as the earth's offspring, the last outward growing product of earth's living organism, the animal world as a whole, should be related to humankind. Children are thus enabled—in a living way—to find their own place in nature and in the world. They begin to understand that the plant world belongs to the earth. On the other hand, we teach them that all the animal species in the world represent, in a sense, the path to human development. Plants are related to the earth, animals to humans; this should be our foundation. I can justify this here only as a principle; the actual details of what one teaches to a child of ten to twelve about the animal world must be worked out with true artistic feeling.

In a way that is simple, even primitive, we first call the children's attention to human nature. This is possible if there is already an artistic foundation. They will come to understand, in a simple way, that people have a threefold organization. First, we have a head, a hard shell that holds the nervous system and the soft parts within it. The head may be compared with the round earth within the cosmos. We do our best to give children concrete, artistic

concepts of the head, then
lead them to the second
member, the rhythmic
system, which includes
the organs for breathing
and blood circulation.

After talking about the
artistic cup-shape of the
skull, which holds the soft parts of the brain, we consider
the series of bones that make up the spinal column and
the branching ribs. We study the characteristics of the
chest and its breathing and circulatory systems. Then we
reach the third member, the metabolism and limbs. As
organs of movement, the limbs are connected with and
maintain the body's metabolism, since their activities regulate the processes of combustion. Limbs and metabolism
must be taken together and constitute the third member
of the human being.

First, then, we establish this human threefold division.
If our teaching is imbued with the necessary artistic feeling, and if it is presented in the form of pictures, one can
communicate this concept of the threefold human being.
Next, we point to the various animal species spread
around the world. We begin with the lowest forms—creatures whose soft organic parts are inside and surrounded
by shell formations. Strictly speaking, certain lower animal species are no more than protoplasm surrounded by
a sheath. We show the children how the human head
appears in a primitive form in these lower creatures. Our
head has the form of a lower animal, transformed to the
highest level of development. The head and, in particular,
the nervous system must not be compared to mammals
or apes, but only to the lowest forms of animal life. We

must go very far back in the earth's history, to the most ancient formations, and there we find animals that appear as a kind of elementary head. We try to explain the lowest animals to children in terms of a primitive head organization.

Then we look at somewhat higher animals—fish and similar species. In them, the spinal column is especially developed, and we explain that these "half-animals" are beings in which the human rhythmic system was developed, the other members being stunted. In the lowest animals, we find an elementary stage corresponding to the human head. In fish-related species, we find an emphasized development of the human system of the chest area.

Finally, the system of limbs and metabolism brings us to the higher animals. The limbs are formed in great diversity in the higher animals. The structures of a horse's hoof, a lion's paw, and the webbed feet of a wader all give us a golden opportunity for artistic description. Or we may compare human limbs to the more extreme development found in apes. In other words, we begin to understand the higher animals by studying the formation of the movement or digestive organs.

Predators differ from the ruminant mammals, since the latter have very long intestinal tracts, whereas in predators the intestinal tract is shorter, while the system connecting the circulatory and digestive processes is powerfully developed. A study of the organization of the higher animals immediately shows how extreme its development is compared to the human system of limbs and metabolism. We can provide a concrete image of how the front part of the spine in an animal is really "head." The digestive system as a whole continues into the head. Essentially, an animal's head belongs to the stomach and intestines. In people, on the other hand, what remained "pristine"—the soft brain and the protective shell of bone—is placed above the limb and metabolic system. The human head is thus raised a stage higher than in the animal, which merely continues the metabolism. Yet, in human beings the head goes back to what, in the simplest way, that system provides: soft substance surrounded by a cuplike, bony formation.

We can also study the jaws of certain animals, showing that they are farthest forward in animals. This is the best way to get a flexible understanding of the head of animals. Human beings emerge as a synthesis of three systems: the head, the chest, and the limbs and metabolism. In each animal, there is an exaggerated development of one of these systems. Thus, we first consider the lower animals such as crustaceans; then mammals, such as birds; and "chest-animals" such as fish, reptiles, and so on, which have a well-developed chest system.

We see that the animal kingdom is, in a sense, a human being separated and fanned out over the earth. We relate the world of the plants to the earth and the myriad animal species to the human being, who is, in fact, a synthesis of the entire animal world. Beginning with human body, we give children, in a simple way, an idea of the threefold nature of our being. Going on to animals, we describe the various species and how there is always an exaggerated development of particular organs, whereas in human beings those organs are united as a harmonious whole. This exaggerated, specialized development manifests in certain animals with the chest organs, in some the lower intestines, and in others the upper organs of digestion. In many forms of animal life (birds, for example), we find that certain organs transformed, such as those for

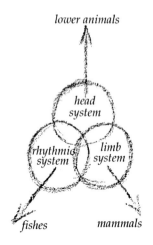

digestion. We can describe how each animal specie represents an extreme development of a human organ system. In a sense, the whole animal world manifests as a human being spread over the earth in diverse forms, with the whole animal kingdom as a synthesis.

We can return to human beings, once we have clearly described the animal world as a "human being" who has exaggerated individual organ systems—with one system living one animal specie, another system as a different specie. This should be done when children approach the twelfth year, for they can then naturally understand that, because we carry spirit within us, as human beings we are an artistic synthesis of our separate parts, otherwise reflected in the various animal species. Because we bear our spirit within us, we can harmonize the lower animal organization into a whole. In a complex way, we transform this into the head system, correspondingly fitted into that of the breast, which we also develop so as to harmonize with the rest. We thus bear within ourselves the fish organization, along with the higher animal organization, arranged harmoniously into a whole. The separate fragments of the human being, scattered over the world in the realm of the animals, are gathered by spirit into a whole being. We relate the human to the animal realm, but we are lifted above animals because we bear spirit.

The purpose of such teaching will be obvious to those who are unbiased. When botany is taught as indicated, it works in the realm of living ideas and places human beings correctly in the world, capable of working and navigating life in an engaged way. And an equally living view of the human relationship to the whole animal world strengthens the will.

Naturally, you can see that what I have discussed here in roughly twenty minutes must be developed gradually over a long time; we must accustom children to unite these ideas with their entire nature. Thus, these ideas will enter each person's role in the world by strengthening the will. The will grows strong when we realize that, by grace of living spirit, we develop as a synthesis of the animal kingdom. This helps form the will.

The goal of our educational work, therefore, is not merely to provide information about the plants and animals, but to develop character—in other words, children's whole human nature. When we teach about plants, we work toward the proper cultivation of intelligence, and we cultivated volition by teaching about animals. In this way, we help children of nine to twelve relate to these other creatures of the earth, so that, through proper intelligence and self-confident will, they may find their way properly through the world.

Above all, in education we must see that human beings develop in relation to both intelligence and volition. Out of feeling, which we have cultivated in children of seven to nine and a half, we develop intelligence and a strong will. Thinking, feeling, and volition are thus harmonized instead of being developed in the usual unnatural way. Everything is rooted in feeling. We must begin with the feelings of children. From their feeling in relation to the world, we cultivate thinking through an understanding of plant, because the life of the plants never allows dead

concepts. Out of feeling, we also develop the will by leading children to what connects them properly with the animal world, while raising children above them.

Thus we work to nurture the appropriate intelligence
and a strong volition in human beings. This is in fact our
primary purpose in education, because only this can
make children fully human, and such development is the
goal of all education.

9

ARITHMETIC, GEOMETRY, HISTORY

August 14, 1923

Arithmetic and geometry, indeed, all mathematics, occupy a unique position in education. Teaching cannot have the necessary vitality and lead to a real interplay between the souls of teachers and students unless teachers fully realize the consequences of what they do and the methods they use. Teachers must know exactly the effect produced by the treatment that children receive in school—or anywhere. We are beings of body, soul, and spirit, and our physical nature is shaped by spirit. Teachers, then, must always be aware of what takes place in the soul and spirit when a change occurs in the body, and again, the physical effect when spirit or soul is affected.

Many things affect a child's imagination, such as painting or drawing, which becomes writing, or botany, when taught as described yesterday. And, above all, we must consider a higher member of our being—one I referred to as the ether body, or the body of formative forces. First, human beings have a physical body. It is perceived by ordinary sensory perception. In addition, we have an inner organization, perceptible only to *imaginative* cognition: a suprasensory, ether body. Further, we have an organization perceptible only to *inspiration*—the next stage of suprasensory knowledge. (These expressions need not confuse us; they are merely terms.) *Inspiration* provides perception of the "astral" body and the I, the true human self.

From birth until death, the ether body of formative forces, the first suprasensory human member, is never separate from the physical body; this happens only at death. During sleep, the ether organization stays in bed with the physical body. While we sleep, the astral body and I-being leave the physical and ether bodies and reenter at the moment of waking. It is the physical and ether bodies that are affected when children are taught arithmetic and geometry, or when we lead them into writing from a foundation of drawing and painting. All this remains and continues to reverberate in the ether body during sleep. On the other hand, history and biology, which I talked about in yesterday's lecture, affects only the astral body and I-being. We take the results of these studies out of the physical and ether bodies and into the spirit world while asleep. After we teach a child plant lore or writing, the effects are held in the physical and ether bodies during sleep and continue to vibrate, whereas the effects of a history lesson on human nature are different, because they are carried out into the spirit world by the I-being and astral body. Thus, the effects vary greatly depending on the lessons.

We have to understand that all impressions given to children that have an imaginative or pictorial quality tend to be perfected during sleep. However, whatever we tell children about history or the human being works on the soul and spirit and tends to be forgotten, losing its quality and growing dim during sleep. In our lessons, therefore, we must determine whether the subject will speak to the ether and physical bodies or to the astral body and I.

Thus, botany and rudimentary writing and reading, which I mentioned yesterday, affect the physical and ether bodies. Everything learned about history (I will speak about teaching this later) or about the human relationship to animals affects the astral body and I-being, the higher members that leave the physical and ether bodies during sleep. The remarkable thing, however, is that arithmetic and geometry affect the physical, ether, and the astral bodies and the I. Arithmetic and geometry are a sort of chameleon; their very nature is to harmonize with every part of our being. Whereas biology and botany lessons should be given at a definite age, arithmetic and geometry should be taught throughout childhood, though, of course, in ways suited to the various stages.

It is most important to remember that the ether body begins to function independently when it is abandoned by the I and astral body. Because of its inherent vibrational forces, it always tends to perfect and elaborate anything brought to it. In terms of our astral body and I, we are stupid, so to speak. Instead of perfecting what has been communicated to these members of our being, we make it less perfect. While asleep, however, our body of formative forces continues, in a suprasensory way, to work with all that it received as arithmetic and the like. We are then no longer in the physical and ether bodies; they continue to calculate or draw geometric figures and perfect them at a suprasensory level. If we are aware of this and plan our teaching accordingly, we can generate great vitality in a child's being. We must, however, make it possible for the ether body to perfect and elaborate what it previously received. In geometry, therefore, we must not begin with abstract, intellectual constructs, which are usually considered the right foundation. We

begin instead with inner perception by stimulating, for example, a strong sense of symmetry in children.

We can begin to do this with even the youngest children. For example, one draws some figure on the blackboard, adds a straight line, and indicates the beginning of symmetry. Then we try to help the children realize that the figure is incomplete and, using every means possible, get them to complete it themselves. Thus, we awaken an inner, active urge to complete what is unfinished. This helps them activate the correct image of a reality. Teachers, of course, must have creative talent, which is always good. Above all, they must have flexible, creative thinking. After assigning these exercises for awhile, the teacher moves on to others. For example, we may draw a figure like this on the blackboard, and try to awaken an inner, spatial impression of it in the children. We then vary the outer line and they gradually learn to draw an inner form corresponding to the outer.

In one, the curves are simple and straightforward. In the other, they curve out at various points. We should explain to the children that, for the sake of inner symmetry, in the inner figure, they should curve inward exactly where the lines curve outward in the outer figure. In the first diagram, a simple line corresponds to another simple line, whereas in the second, an inward curve corresponds to an outward curve.

Or, we may draw something like this, followed by corresponding outer forms, so that we make a harmonious whole. We now try to move from this to another exercise, in which we do not let the outer figures come together but make them run away from each other into the "undefined." The children get the impression that this point wants to move off, and perhaps one has to chase after it

with these lines but cannot catch it; it got away. Then they realize that the corresponding figure must be arranged so that, because *this* ran away, *that* must be especially bent inward. (I can only suggest these principles.) Briefly, by working like this, we give children an idea of "asymmetrical symmetry," thus preparing the ether body during waking life so that it continues to vibrate during sleep. And, in those vibrations, it perfects what has been absorbed during the day. Then the children awake in an ether body—as well as a physical body—inwardly and naturally stimulated to activity. They will be filled with life and vitality. This cannot be achieved, of course, unless the teacher has some knowledge of the ether body's activity; if such knowledge is not present, any effort in this way will be mechanical and superficial.

True teachers are concerned not only with the waking life, but also with events during sleep. In this sense, it is important to understand certain things that occasionally happen to all of us. For example, we think over some problem in the evening and fail to find a solution. In the morning, however, the problem is resolved. Why? Because the ether body of formative forces continued its activity independently during the night.

In many respects, waking life is not a process that perfects, but one that disturbs. We need to leave our physical and ether bodies alone for awhile so that we do not make them stupid through the activities of the astral body and I. Many things in life substantiate this fact; using the example just mentioned, when you wake up in the morning, you might feel slightly restless, but you suddenly discover that the solution came to you unconsciously during the night. These things are mere stories; they happen just as conclusively as any experiment. What occurred in this particular case? The work of the ether body continued through the night, and you were asleep the whole time. This is not normal or something to strive for. But we should strive to help that etheric activity continue during sleep, and we do this when we begin by communicating a concrete representation of space, instead of beginning geometry with triangles and the like, in which the intellect is already in evidence. In arithmetic, too, we must proceed in this way.

A pamphlet on physics and mathematics by Dr. von Baravalle (a teacher at the Waldorf school) gives a good idea of how to bring concrete reality into math and geometry. The pamphlet also extends this whole way of thinking into the realm of physics, although it deals primarily with higher mathematics. If we go into its underlying spirit, it is a wonderful guide for teaching math in a way that corresponds to the natural needs of a child's being. It created a starting point for stimulating reform in the method of teaching mathematics and physics, from early childhood to the highest levels of instruction. We must be able to take what the pamphlet says about concrete concepts of space and extend it to arithmetic.

The whole point is that everything arithmetic conveys externally to children, even counting, destroys something in the human organism. To begin with a unit and add to it, piece by piece, merely destroys the human organism. But the organism is made more alive when we begin by awakening an awareness of the whole, then awakening an awareness of the members of that whole; we begin with the whole and proceed to its parts. This must be kept in mind, even when children are learning to count. Usually, we learn to count by observing purely physical, external things. We begin with 1, a unity, then add 2, 3, 4, and so on, unit by unit—and we have absolutely no idea why one follows the other, or what happens in the end. We are taught to count through an arbitrary juxtaposition of units. I am well aware that there are many methods for teaching children to count, but very little attention is paid to the principle of starting with the whole and proceeding to the parts. Children should first see the unit as a whole. Everything is a unity, no matter what it is.

Here we have to illustrate this with a drawing. We must therefore draw a line; but we could use an apple just as well to do what I am doing with a line. This, then, is 1. Now we go from the whole to the parts, or members. Thus,

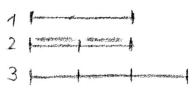

we have made a *1* into a *2,* but the *1* still remains. The unit has been divided into two. Thus we come to the *2.* And we continue, and another partition brings the *3* into being. Unity always remains the all-embracing whole. And so we go, through *4, 5,* and so on. Moreover, at the same time, using another means, we can give an idea of how well we are able to hold in the mind everything that relates to number, and we discover just how limited we are in our power of mental presentation when it comes to numbers.

In some countries today, the concept of number that is clearly held in the mind's eye goes only up to ten. Here in England, money is counted up to twelve. But that really represents the maximum of what is mentally visualized, because in reality we then begin again and repeat the numbers. For example, we count up to ten, then we begin counting the tens, *2 x 10 = 20,* and *3 x 10 = 30.* Here we no longer consider the things themselves but begin to calculate the number itself, whereas the more elementary concept requires things themselves to be clearly present in the mind.

People are proud of the fact that they use very advanced methods to count, compared to primitive people, who depend on their ten fingers. But there is little basis for such pride. We count to ten because we feel the members of our hands. We feel our two hands and ten fingers symmetrically. Children also experience this feeling, and we must evoke the sense of number through transition from the whole to the parts. Then we easily find another transition, which leads us to counting, in which we add to another. Eventually, of course, we can move on to the ordinary *1, 2, 3,* and so on. But merely adding one or more units together must not be introduced until the second level, for it has significance only in physical space, whereas dividing a unity into members has an inner meaning that continues to vibrate in a child's ether body, even when we are no longer present. It is important that we know such things.

After teaching children to count in this way, something else becomes important. We must not proceed to addition in a dead, mechanical way, by merely adding one item to another in series. Life arises when we begin not with parts of addition, but with the whole total. We begin  with a number of objects; for example, you throw down a number of little balls. We've gone far enough in counting to say there are fourteen balls. You divide them up, extending the concept of parts even further. You have five here, four there, and five again. You have separated the total into 5 + 4 + 5. We go from the total to the units that comprise it, from the whole to the parts. The method we should use with children is to set up the total for them first, and then let the children perceive how the given total can be divided up. This is very important. One does not harness a horse with its tail to the front; likewise, when teaching arithmetic, we must go the right way. We start from a whole actually present in the total—a reality—and then separate it into parts; later, we find our way back to the ordinary sum total.

Continuing in this way, from a living whole to separate parts, one touches the reality behind all mathematical calculations: the vibration of the ether body of formative forces. This body needs a living stimulus for its formative, perfecting activity, which it continues with no need for the presence of the astral body and I-being and their disturbing elements.

Your teaching will be essentially enhanced and vivified if, in a similar way, you reverse the other simple forms of calculation. Today, one might say, children are upside down and must righted. For example, try to get a child to think in this way: "If I have seven, how much must I take away to get three?" instead of "What is left after I take four away from seven?" Having seven is the real thing, and what I have left is equally real; how much must we take away from seven to get three? Beginning with this kind of thinking, we stand in the middle of life, whereas with the opposite form we face an abstraction. Proceeding this way, we can easily revert to the other eventually.

Thus, again, in multiplication and division, we should not ask what will result when we divide ten into two parts, but how must we divide ten to get five. The actual aspect is given; in life, eventually we want to get to something with real significance. Here are two children; ten apples will be divided among them. Each is supposed to get five. These are realities. What we must first contribute is the abstract part in the middle.

When we do things this way, things are directly adapted to life, and, if we are successful, the usual, purely external way of adding by counting one thing after another with a deadening effect on the arithmetic lessons will instead become a vivifying force of particular importance in this area of educational work. We must really consider the subconscious aspect of human beings—that is, the part that not only continues to work during sleep, but also works subconsciously during the waking hours. We do not always think of everything. We are aware of only a small fragment of our soul's experience, but the rest is always active. Let's create the possibility for children's physical and ether bodies to work in a healthy way, recognizing that we can do so only when we bring atmosphere, interest, and life into our lessons in arithmetic and geometry.

A question has been raised during this conference about whether it is truly a good thing to continue teaching subjects for certain blocks of time, as we do in a Waldorf school. The right division of lessons into periods is the most fruitful. "Block" teaching means that one lesson will never encroach on another. Instead of setting up daily schedules with definite hours—arithmetic from 8 to 9; history, religion, or whatever from 9 to 10—we give one main lesson on the same subject for two hours every morning for three to five weeks. Then we move on to another main lesson for perhaps five or six weeks on another subject, which, if you like, develops from the previous work, but is again taught for those two hours. The children thus concentrate on one subject for some weeks.

It was asked if this might not have the result that children forget too much of what they had been taught. If the lessons have been taught properly, however, the previous subject will continue to work in the subconscious during the next subject. In "block" lessons, we are always dealing with the subconscious processes in children. There is nothing more fruitful than to allow the results of the lessons during one period to rest in the soul and continue to work in a person without interference. It will soon be apparent that, when a subject has been taught correctly, when it's time to take it up again for another period and it is recalled to mind, it emerges very differently than it would have had it been taught poorly. One ignores the factors at work by arguing that, because a subject might be forgotten, it isn't right to teach this way. We must naturally deal with the possibility of forgetting, for just consider all we would have to carry in our heads if we could not forget and then remember again. The role of forgetting, therefore, as well as the actual instruction, must be factored into real education.

I am not saying that we should rejoice when children forget; we can safely leave that to them. Everything depends on what passes into the subconscious in a way that enables it to be recalled. The subconscious belongs to our being as much as the conscious. In all these matters, we must realize that the purpose of education is to appeal both to the whole person and to that individual's various members. Again, it is essential to begin with the whole; first, there must be an understanding of the whole, and then the parts. First we grasp the whole, and then the parts. If we count merely by placing one object next to another and then adding them up, we eliminate the wholeness of being human. We appeal to the whole human being by first visualizing the total as a whole and then proceeding to the parts that make it up.

When we teach history, we are open to the danger of losing sight of the human being. We have seen that in a truly beneficial education, we must give everything its proper place. Plants must be studied in connection with the earth, and the various animal species in connection with humankind. Whatever the subject, the concrete human element must be retained; everything must be related, in some way, to the human being.

When we begin to teach history, we must be aware that, although children at this age can see the connection between plants and the earth and see the earth itself as an organism, and they can see the human being as a living synthesis of the whole animal kingdom, these children cannot form any real ideas of "causal connections" in history. In an ordinary sense, we may be very skillful at teaching history, describing one age after another and show how the first causes the second, and we may describe the history of art and how Michelangelo followed Leonardo da Vinci in a natural sequence of cause and effect, but before the age of twelve, children do not understand cause and effect, which is a conventional factor when adults study history. Just as merely pounding on a piano has no meaning, this way of teaching history means nothing to children, and it is only through coercion that they will take it in at all. Its effect on their souls is like one eating a stone. We would not dream of giving one's stomach a stone instead of bread, and likewise we must also nourish the soul with food it can assimilate, not with stones. If history is to be communicated in a living way to people, we must first awaken a concept of time that is connected to the human being.

We might have three history books, one on antiquity, another on the Middle Ages, and yet another on modern history, but there would be little sense of time in them. But suppose I begin by telling the students, "You are ten years old, so you were alive in 1913. Your father is much older than you, and he was alive in 1890, and his father was alive in 1850. Now imagine stretching your arm back to your father, who stretches his arm back to his father, your grandfather. Now you have reached back to 1850." The students then begin to realize that three or four generations represent just about one century. The generations run backward from the twentieth century and bring students to their very early ancestors. Therefore, the sixtieth generation of ancestors leads to the era of Christ's birth. If the classroom is large enough, it may be possible to arrange the children in a line and have them stretch their arms from one to another, so that the sixtieth child represents an ancestor living at the time of Christ's birth. Space thus becomes time.

Teachers who have fertile, inventive minds will find other ways to express this; I am merely suggesting a principle. In this way, children begin to see that they are part of history; people such as Alfred the Great, Cromwell, and others are made to seem as though they were ancestors. All of history becomes a part of life at school when it is presented as a living concept of time.

History must never be separated from human beings. Children must not see it as just so much book learning. Many people seem to think that history is contained in books, although it's not always quite that bad. In any case, we must use every possible way to awaken a sense of history that lives, with human beings in its flow.

Once a living view of time has been awakened, we can begin to imbue history with life and soul, just as we did for arithmetic and geometry by developing living perception. There is a lot of quibbling today about the nature of perception, but the whole point is that we must develop living, not dead, perception. In the symmetry exercises I described, the soul lives within the act of perception. This is living perception. Our goal is to awaken a living perception of space, and by teaching history in a living way to children of nine to twelve, we fill them with an element that arises from the inner qualities of heart and soul, not merely from the nature of space.

History lessons must be permeated thoroughly with a quality of the heart. Thus, we present it as much as possible through images. Students must see real forms, and these must never be described with cool detachment. One's descriptions must be colored with both morality and religious feeling, without making the mistake of using them as examples for moral or religious admonition. Above all, history must take hold of the students' feeling and will. They must be able to experience a personal relationship with historical individuals and ways of life in the various eras. Nor do we need to limit ourselves to describing people. We could describe the life of a twelfth-century town, but whatever we say must go into the feelings and volition of the children. They must be able to "live" the events, thus forming themselves within them by arousing their own sympathies and antipathies, because their feelings and will are stimulated.

This shows that we must always bring the element of art into our history lessons. Art comes into play when (as I often describe it) we exercise true economy in teaching. This economy can be exercised when teachers have thoroughly mastered the subject before entering the classroom; one no longer needs to think it over, because, if prepared properly, the subject is present in a flexible way for the teacher's soul. Teachers must be so well prepared that the only thing left to do is to shape the lesson in an artistic way. The problem of teaching is thus not just a matter of interest, diligence, and devotion on the part of the students, but mostly on the part of the teacher. Lessons should never be presented until they have been deeply experienced within the teacher's spirit. Of course, the faculty must be organized so that the teachers have enough time to fully and intensely experience the lessons.

It's terrible to see teachers walking with books among their students as they wrestle with the subject. Those who fail to see how wrong this is in terms of true educational principles are also unaware of what occurs subconsciously in the children's souls, nor are they aware of the terrible effects of such an experience. If we teach history out of notebooks, children come to a certain conclusion—not consciously, but subconsciously. The unconscious, intellectual conclusion, rooted deeply in a child's organism, is this: Why should one learn all these things? The teacher doesn't know them and must use notes. Anyone can do that, so there is no need to learn them.

Of course, children do not reach this conclusion consciously. Nevertheless, judgments have even greater force when rooted in the subconscious life of heart and feeling. Our lessons must vibrate with inner vitality and freshness from the teacher's own being. When describing historical persons, for example, teachers should not have to make an effort to remember dates. I already described how we should communicate a concept of time through an image of successive generations. Another aspect is this: *when teaching history, it must flow with elemental force from the teacher.* It must never be abstract; the teacher, as a human being, must be the vital factor.

It has been said many times that education should affect the whole human being, not just one aspect. While, it is important to consider what subjects children need to learn and whether we need to focus more on their intellect or their will, the question of a teacher's work is just as important. When it is a matter of educating the whole human being, teachers must be "human" in the fullest sense of the word—not those teaching is based merely on mechanical memory and facts, but teach out of their own being. That is the real essence.

10

PHYSICS, CHEMISTRY, HANDWORK, LANGUAGE, RELIGION

August 15, 1923

From what I have said about how to teach children about nature, plants, and animals, you probably realize that the aim of a Waldorf school is to relate educational methods to the evolutionary laws and forces as they operate through the stages of a child's development. I spoke of the significant turning point between the ninth and tenth years, when children begin to distinguish themselves from the world. Before that age, in their thinking and feeling there is no sense of separation between themselves and the world's phenomena. Until the ninth year, therefore, we must speak of plants, animals, mountains, rivers, and such in the language of fairy tales, appealing above all to children's fantasy. Animals, plants, and springs must speak, so that the same kind of being that children are first aware of in themselves also speaks to them out of the external world.

Keep in mind how we lead children at this age into botany and zoology, and you will realize that the goal is to bring children into the right relationship with the world around them. They come to know plants in connection with the earth and study them from this point of view. The earth becomes a living being who produces the plants, just as a human head produces hair through a vital principle within it—although plant forms of the earth have a much richer life and variety. This relationship with the plant world and with the whole earth is of great value to the well-being of a child's body and soul. If we teach children to see humanity as a synthesis of the animal species spread out over the earth, we help them find a truer relationship with the lower creatures. Before eleven or twelve, the common thread of all nature study should be this relation of humankind to the world.

Then comes the age when, for the first time, we may show children the world's outer processes independently of human beings. Between eleven and twelve, and not until then, we may begin to teach about minerals and stones. Plants, as they grow out of the earth, are related in this sense to stones and minerals. Earlier teaching about the mineral kingdom in any other form than this seriously harms child's inner flexibility of soul. Anything that has no relationship with humankind is, by nature, mineral. We should begin to deal with the mineral kingdom only after children have properly found their place in the world—when in thinking and, especially, in feeling they have grasped the life of the plants, and when the will has been strengthened by a true view of animals. These are the two kingdoms of nature closest to children.

What applies to the minerals applies equally to physics and chemistry, and to the "causal" connections of history and geography—in other words, to any process that must be studied as separate from humankind. Any study of the great historical connections that cannot be related directly to human beings (as I described yesterday) should be delayed until the eleventh or twelfth year. Only then can we begin to study subjects that have little to do with the human.

The right age for children to begin school is around the time of the second teeth, at about seven. Until then, school is not really the place for them; to take a child before this age requires all kinds of compromises. I will try to explain certain basic principles. When children first come to school, our teaching accommodates the fact that, as yet, they do not distinguish between themselves and the world at large. When the children are between nine and ten, we begin to awaken a living intelligence through knowledge of plants, and strengthen their will through knowledge of animals. In mineralogy, physics, and chemistry we can work only on the intellect, and then, as a necessary counterbalance, we introduce art (I will say more about this tomorrow). From eleven or twelve on, we find that children are able to form logical concepts of cause and effect, and this must be elaborated through physics and chemistry. But those processes (which should lead gradually to astronomy) must not be explained to children before they reach eleven or twelve. Before then, if we describe simple chemical processes—say, combustion—we must use pure imagery, with no reference to the logic of cause and effect, which should not be introduced until they reach eleven or twelve. The less we say about causality before then, the stronger and more vital and more inward will the soul become; if, on the other hand, we introduce causality to younger children, dead concepts and even dead feelings enter the soul and have a withering effect.

The goal of Waldorf methods has always been to create a plan that works out of the human being. In every detail, we consider the various life stages and fit the lessons to the needs of human nature itself. On the other hand, it is always our intention to enable children to enter life in the world in the right way. To do this, we must lead from physics and chemistry into various forms of practical work for children who have reached fourteen or fifteen. In classes for these children, therefore, we introduce hand spinning and weaving. These activities lead children intelligently into practical life. Our students learn spinning and weaving and become familiar with how these things are done in a factory. They should also have some knowledge of basic chemical technology, the preparation and manufacture of dyes, and similar processes.

During school, children should acquire truly practical concepts of their environment. The affairs of ordinary life often remain a mystery to many people today, because the education they receive does not lead, at the right time, from what is essentially human to life's practical activities in the world. In a sense, this will certainly harm the soul's development. Consider the human body's sensitivity to some element in the air that it cannot assimilate. In society, of course, conditions are somewhat different. There we are forced to put up with many incongruities, but we can adapt ourselves if we have been introduced to them at the right age and in the right way.

Consider how many people there are today who get into a train without the faintest idea of how it operates or what makes it move. They see a train every day and have absolutely no idea of the mechanics of a locomotive. This means that people are surrounded by inventions of the human mind, but have no contact at all with them. It is the beginning of an antisocial life simply to accept inventions of the human mind without at least understanding them in a general way. In a Waldorf school, therefore, when the children reach fourteen or fifteen, we provide instruction and experience in matters that play a role in practical life. Today, the age of adolescence is regarded from a very limited, slanted perspective. In fact, human beings open up to the world at puberty. Previously, children lived more internally, but now they are ready to understand other people and the world's phenomena. So, we act according to the principles of human development when, before children reach puberty, we concentrate on all that relates the human to nature. But, at the age of fourteen or fifteen, we must focus our energy on connecting children with the inventions of the human mind. This helps them understand and find their place in society. If educators had followed this principle sixty or seventy years ago, today's "social movement" would have taken a very different form in Europe and America. There has been tremendous progress in technological and commercial efficiency during the last sixty or seventy years. There has been real progress in technical skills, national trade has become world trade, and a global economy has grown out of national economies. In the past sixty or seventy years, the outer appearance of society has been transformed, yet our educational methods have continued as though nothing happened. We have completely neglected to familiarize children with the practical affairs of the world at the age when this should be done, at the age of fourteen or fifteen.

At Waldorf schools, we are not so narrow-minded that we in any way belittle higher classical education, because for in many ways it is very useful; for students who desire it or whose parents desire it, we prepare them both for a higher classical education and for final certificates and diplomas. But we never forget today's need to understand why the Greeks—whose singular purpose in education was to serve practical life—did not spend all their time learning Egyptian, a language of the distant past, whereas today we make a special point of teaching our boys, as well as girls, not about the present but about a world of the past. It's no wonder that most people have so little understanding of how to live in the world today. The world's destiny is now beyond human control, simply because education has not kept pace with changing social conditions.

In Waldorf schools, we follow our feeling that we can indeed help our students develop fully as human beings and find their place in the ranks of humankind. This must be our primary consideration when teaching languages. As far as the children's native tongue is concerned, of course, our teaching is adapted to the child's age; we teach as I have already described in relation to other lessons. An outstanding feature of language instruction, however, is that at a Waldorf school we begin teaching two foreign languages, French and English, as soon as children begin school at six or seven. Thus we try to give them something that will become increasingly necessary in the future.

To understand the purely human aspect of teaching languages, keep in mind that the faculty of speech is rooted in the very depths of our being. Native language is so deeply rooted in the breathing, blood circulation, and vascular system that the way the mother tongue is expressed in children affects them not only in spirit and soul, but also physically. We must realize, however, that the world's different languages permeate human beings and express the human element in various ways. This is quite obvious in the case of primitive languages. And it is true of the more civilized languages, though this often escapes notice.

There is one European language that arises purely from the element of feeling. With time, intellectualism has taken hold of its element of feeling, but feeling is nevertheless the basis of that language; hence, the elements of intellect and will are less firmly implanted in the human being through that language itself. By studying other languages, the elements of will and intellect must be developed. And there is another language that emanates particularly from the element of formative fantasy; the configuration of the sounds themselves carry everything. Because of this, children acquire an innately formative power as they learn to speak. Another language in civilized Europe is rooted mainly in the element of will. Its very cadences, vowels, and consonants reveal this. When people speak, it's as though they were driving back the ocean's waves with exhaled air. The element of volition lives in that language. Other languages evoke more the elements of feeling, music, or imagination. Each language is related to the human being in a particular way. You will probably say that I should name these languages, but I purposely avoid that, because we have not reached the point where we can face civilization with the objectivity needed to bear the impersonal truth of such matters.

From what I have said about the nature of various languages, you can understand that the way one particular genius of language affects human nature must be balanced by the effects of another—that is, if our goal is truly human and not nationalistic. This is why a Waldorf school begins with three languages, even for the very youngest children; we devote a great deal of time to this subject. It is good to begin teaching foreign languages at this early age, because, up to nine or ten years of age, children still carry some of the qualities of the first period of life, from birth to the change of teeth. During those years, children are mostly imitative. They learn their native language completely by imitating. Without much demand on the intellect, children imitate the language around them, and, at the same time, learn not only the outer sounds of speech, but also the inner, musical, soul element of the language. Their first language is acquired (if I may be allowed the expression) as a finer kind of habit, which passes into the depths of the whole being.

When children come to school after the change of teeth, language lessons appeal more to the soul and less to physical nature. Nevertheless, until nine or ten, children bring with them enough imaginative imitation to enable us to teach a language so that it will be absorbed by their whole being, not just by their forces of soul and spirit. This is why it is so important not to let the first three years of school slip by without foreign language instruction. On purely pedagogical principles, we begin foreign language lessons in a Waldorf school as soon as children enter the elementary classes.

I hardly need to say that teaching languages must be closely adapted to the children's ages. People's thinking today has become chaotic in relation to reality. Because of their materialism, people imagine they are firmly rooted in reality, whereas they are really theorists. Those who are proud of being practical are mainly theoretical; people get it into their heads that something is right, but fail to form it within the context of real life. And so, especially in education, they become unrealistically radical and go to the opposite extreme when they find something wrong. It has been found that, when language lessons (especially Latin and Greek) are based entirely on grammar and syntax, they tend to become mechanical and superficial. As a result, exactly the opposite principle has been applied, simply because thinking is not consistent. People see that something is incorrect and go to the other extreme, thinking that this will correct the problem. The result is that now they employ the principle of teaching no grammar at all. This is irrational, because it means only that, in one area of knowledge, one is left at the level of mere awareness and not allowed to advance to self-awareness. Between the ninth and tenth years, children go from the level of awareness to self-awareness; they distinguish themselves from the world.

At this age, we can begin (gradually, of course) teaching grammar and syntax rules, because the children are reaching a point where they think not only about the world, but also about themselves. As far as speech is concerned, thinking about oneself means not merely being able to speak instinctively, but also being able to apply rational rules in language. It makes no sense, therefore, to teach language with no grammar at all. By avoiding rules altogether, we cannot give children the necessary inner firmness for life's tasks. It is most important to keep in mind that children do not pass willingly from awareness to self-awareness until nine or ten. To teach grammar before then is absolutely irrational.

We must be able to recognize the change that occurs around nine or ten, so that we can lead children gradually from an instinctive, direct acquisition of language into the rational aspect of grammar. This also applies to a child's native language. We do real harm to children's souls if they are crammed full of grammatical and syntactical rules before this important turning point in their lives. Speech should be a matter of instinct and habit, learned solely through imitation. It is the purpose of language to inaugurate self-awareness between nine and ten—and as a rule self-awareness comes to light in grammar and syntax. This is why Waldorf education uses the two or three preceding years to introduce language lessons at the right age according to the principles of human development.

Perhaps you see why Waldorf education aims to gradually enable teachers to read the human being as such—not according to books or the rules of an educational system. Waldorf teachers must learn to read the human being—the most wonderful document in the world. From this reading, teachers develop a deep enthusiasm for teaching, because only the contents of the "book of the world" can stimulate the overall activity of body, soul, and spirit needed by teachers. Any book study should be a means of enabling teachers to read the great book of the world. Teachers who can do this will teach with the necessary enthusiasm, and only such enthusiasm can generate the energetic impulse that brings life into classrooms.

The principle of the "universal human" (I described this in terms of various areas of education) is expressed by Waldorf education. It does not in any way promote a particular philosophy or religious conviction. In this sense, as an art of education derived from spiritual science, it has been absolutely essential for Waldorf schools to remove any hint of being "anthroposophic schools." They absolutely cannot be anything of the sort. There must be daily efforts to avoid falling into anthroposophic biases, shall we say, because of excessive enthusiasm and honest conviction on the part of teachers. Such conviction is present in the Waldorf teachers, of course, because they are anthroposophists. But the fundamental question of Waldorf education is the human being as such, not human beings as followers of any particular philosophy.

Therefore, with the various religious denominations in mind, we were willing to compromise with today's needs, and, early on, we focused on educational methods based on the "universal human." First of all, religious instruction was left to the pastors—Catholicism to Catholic priests, Protestantism to Protestant ministers. But a great many pupils in the Waldorf school are "dissenters" (as we call them in Central Europe), children who wished to receive no religious instruction if it were limited to Catholicism and Protestant teaching. Waldorf education was originally developed for the children of working people connected with a certain business, though for some time now, the school has been there for children at all economic levels. Consequently, most of the children had no religious affiliation. As frequently happens in Central European schools, those children were taught nothing in terms of religion, and so, for their sake, we introduced "free" religious instruction.

We never try to introduce theoretical spiritual science into the school; this would be absolutely incorrect. Thus far, spiritual science has been presented to adults, and its ideas and concepts are thus clothed in a way suited to them. Merely to take anthroposophic literature intended for adults and introduce that to children would distort the whole principle of Waldorf education. And for those children who came to us voluntarily for free religious instruction, the whole point was to give them the religious instruction appropriate for their ages.

Let me say it again: religious teaching at a Waldorf school, as well as the services connected with it, does not in any way try to introduce an anthroposophic worldview, and the children's ages are always considered. Indeed, most of the children attend, although we made it a strict rule to admit only those children whose parents wish it. Because pure pedagogy plays such a central role in our free religious instruction (which is, of course, Christian in the deepest sense), parents who wish their children to be educated according to the Waldorf principles, and in a Christian way, send them to us be educated. As I say, the teaching is thoroughly Christian, with the result that the whole school is pervaded by a deeply Christian atmosphere. Our religious instruction makes the children realize the significance of all the great Christian festivals of Christmas and Easter, for instance, much more deeply than is common today.

The children's ages must be considered in any teaching of religion, because untold harm arises when ideas and views are communicated prematurely. In a Waldorf school, students are led first to understand universal divinity in the world. You will recall that when children first come to school between seven and ten, we let plants, clouds, springs, and such speak for themselves. The children's whole environment is alive and articulate. From this, we can easily lead into the universal and imminent father principle in the world. When the rest of teaching takes the form I described, children can easily conceive that all things have a divine origin.

Thus we form a link with the knowledge of nature conveyed to children through fantasy and fairy tales. The goal is to awaken, first of all, a sense of gratitude for everything in the world. Gratitude for what others do for us and for the gifts of nature; this guides children's religious feeling along the right path. It is tremendously important and meaningful to develop a child's sense of gratitude. It may seem odd, but it is a profound fact that people should learn to feel gratitude whenever the weather is favorable to our endeavors. Being able to feel gratitude to the cosmos—though only in one's imagination—deepens all our feelings in a religious sense.

Love for all of creation must then be added to this sense of gratitude. If we lead children in this way through the age of nine or ten, it becomes very easy to reveal the qualities they must learn to love in the living world around them. Love for each flower, for sunlight, for rain all deepen their perception of the world in a religious sense. If gratitude and love have been awakened in children before the age of ten, we can then develop a true sense and understanding of duty. A true inner religious feeling will never arise from a premature development of the sense of duty through commands and rules.

Those who want to educate in the sense of true Christianity must realize that it is impossible to convey to children's souls, before nine or ten years of age, any understanding of the Mystery of Golgotha and what it brought into the world, nor anything related the person and divinity of Jesus Christ. Children are exposed to great harm, however, if we fail to introduce the principle of universal divinity before this age, and by "universal divinity" I mean the divine father principle. We must show children the divinity in all nature, in all human evolution, and how it lives and moves not only in rocks, but also in the hearts of others and in their every act. Children must be taught, through the natural authority of the teacher, to feel gratitude and love for this universal divinity. Thus, for children of nine and ten, we provide a basis for the right attitude toward the Mystery of Golgotha.

You see now why it is so important to understand the human being in terms of chronological development. Just try to see what a difference it makes whether we teach children of seven or eight about the New Testament, or, having cultivated an awareness of universal divinity in nature, wait until the age of nine and a half or ten before teaching the New Testament. If we do the latter, the children have been prepared, and the Gospels will live in all their suprasensory grandeur. If we teach the New Testament to younger children, it will not take hold of their whole being but remain mere words and rigid, prosaic concepts. The danger is that the children's religious feeling will harden and remain rigid throughout life, instead of living in a way that thoroughly pervades their feeling toward the world. For children of nine or ten onward, we prepare them most wonderfully to receive the glory of Christ if they have already been introduced to the principle of universal divinity that pervades the world.

This, then, is the goal of religious teaching as given in a Waldorf school, where there is an ever-increasing number of children whose parents wish it. The teaching is based on a purely human element and associated with a particular form of ritual. A service is held each Sunday for the children who are given free religious instruction. And for those who have left school, there is a service with a different ritual. A certain ritual, in many ways similar to Mass, is adapted to the children's ages and associated with the religious teaching at the Waldorf school.

There is a principle that we wish to develop at the Waldorf school, and it was very difficult to introduce this into the religious instruction. It is the principle of human as such, and in religious matters today, people are not at all inclined to relinquish their own particular view. We hear much talk about a religion of the "universal human," but most opinions are influenced by the views of a particular religious denomination. If we really understand the purpose of humanity in the future, we will also realize that free religious education as taught at a Waldorf school truly helps in this. Spiritual science, as given to adults, is never brought into a Waldorf school. Instead, we consider it our task to imbue our teaching with the object of human thirst and longing: a realization of the divine in nature and in human history, which arises from a true understanding of the Mystery of Golgotha.

To this end, we give all our teaching the necessary quality and coloring. I have already said that teachers must reach a point where all their work becomes moral activity, and they regard the lessons themselves as a kind of divine office. This can be done only when it is possible to introduce elements of moral instruction and religion for those who desire it, and we have attempted to do this through the religious instruction at the Waldorf school—at least, to the degree that today's society allows. In no sense do we work toward a blind, rationalistic Christianity, but toward a real understanding of the Christ impulse in human evolution. Our only goal is to give people what they need, even after all their other teaching has endowed them with the qualities of full humanity. Even when this is the case—if full humanity has been developed through the other teaching—a religious deepening is still needed before people can find, in a general sense, a place in the world appropriate to their inherent spiritual nature. To develop whole human beings and to deepen them in a true religious sense is considered one of the most essential tasks of Waldorf education.

MEMORY, TEMPERAMENTS,
PHYSICAL EDUCATION, ART

August 16, 1923

There are two aspects we must consider in education. One is related to lesson subjects, and the other relates to the children, whose faculties we must develop according to knowledge based on true observation of the human being. If we adopt the methods described in these lectures, our teaching will always appeal to the particular faculties that should develop during the various stages of life. We must pay special attention, however, to the development of memory in children.

Here it must be realized that, because they lacked a certain understanding of human nature, our predecessors tended to burden the memories of children, and (as I said yesterday in another connection) there has been a tendency to go to the opposite extreme. Most modern systems of education tend to ignore memory almost entirely. Both methods are incorrect. The point is that memory should be left alone before the change of teeth, at which point children generally begin school. I said that, during this period of life, the physical body, ether body, astral body, and I-being work as a unit. The way children develop through imitating everything they observe around them stimulates—even within the physical body itself—the forces that develop memory. Thus, during these childhood years, memory must be allowed to develop without interference.

After the change of teeth, however, when the element of soul and spirit is, in a sense, released from the body, it is very important to train the memory in a systematic way. Throughout our lives, memory places demands on our physical bodies. Unless there is an overall development of the physical body, memory will be impaired. Indeed, it is well known that many kinds of head injuries lead directly to defective memory.

With children, it is not enough to notice that an element of soul is involved in disease. As teachers, we must always be alert to every little effect that soul and spirit produce in the children's physical nature. Overdeveloping the memory will harm a child for the rest of life—even the physical body. So how do we develop a child's memory correctly? Most important, we must realize that abstract concepts developed by the rational intellect overload the memory, especially during the phase of life between the change of teeth and puberty. As I have shown, however, vividly imaginative and perceptible ideas in the lessons—formed artistically as images—awaken living forces that affect even the physical body, allowing memory to develop properly. The best foundation for developing the memory is to teach artistically during the early school years.

If art is taught properly, proper control of physical movement will always result. And by stimulating children to inner activity in art—if their physical nature is stimulated along with qualities of spirit as they paint, write, make music, or draw—we properly develop the soul forces that aid memory in the physical body. (In tomorrow's lecture I will explain how we do this through eurythmy.) We must not make the mistake of believing that we can ever help children by completely ignoring or undernourishing the memory.

There are three golden rules for the developing memory: concepts load the memory; the perceptible arts build it up; activities of will strengthen it and make it firm. We are given wonderful opportunities to apply these three golden rules when we teach nature and history as suggested in these lectures. Arithmetic, too, may be used for this, because even here we should always begin with an artistic feeling, as I tried to show. When children thoroughly understand the simpler operations—say, counting to ten or twenty—there is no need to worry about allowing them to memorize the rest. It is incorrect to overload children with too many concrete pictures, just as it is incorrect to strain their powers of memory, because when concepts become too complex, they have the same effect. We must carefully observe how memory develops in each individual child.

So, we can see the need for teachers to have some understanding of human tendencies toward health or illness. Strange experiences often arise in this connection. A gentleman whose whole thought is concerned with education once came to visit the Waldorf school, and I tried to explain the spirit behind its education. After awhile, he said, "If you work in this way, the teachers will have to know a great deal about medicine." To him, it seemed impossible that teachers could acquire the necessary medical knowledge. I told him that, although this would arise naturally from their knowledge of human nature, a certain amount of medical instruction should be part of any teaching course. Concerns about health should not be left only to a school doctor. It seems we are especially fortunate that our Waldorf school doctor is also part of the college of teachers. Dr. Eugen Kolisko is a doctor by profession, and, in addition to caring for the children's health, he is a member of the teaching staff. In this way everything connected with the children's physical health is harmonized fully with their education.

In effect, our teachers must come to understand the health and illnesses of children. For example, a teacher might notice a child growing pale. Another child's face is becoming excessively red. Teachers who observe accurately will find that the second child shows signs of growing restless and fretful. Such symptoms are related to the soul and spirit. Abnormal pallor—even a tendency—is caused by overworking the memory. The memory of this child has been stressed, and this must be stopped. The memory of the child with too much color, on the other hand, is underworked. This child must be given things to memorize and made to demonstrate that they have been retained. We must relieve the memory of a child growing pale, whereas we must develop the memory a child with excessive color.

The only way we can deal with the whole human being is by handling the nature of soul and spirit in close harmony with the physical body. In a Waldorf school, the children, as growing human beings, are handled according to their individual qualities of spirit, soul, and body, and above all, according to the particular temperament.

We arrange children in the classroom so that the various temperaments—choleric, sanguine, melancholic, and phlegmatic—are expressed and adjusted among themselves. The best technique is to have the choleric and melancholic children sit together, because they tend to temper one another. Of course, we must know how to assess and then deal with the various temperaments, because this is at the root of physical development.

Consider sanguine children, who tend not to pay attention during lessons. Each impression from the outer world directly engages the attention, but passes away just as quickly. The proper treatment for such children is to reduce the amount of sugar in their food, though not too much, of course. The less sugar such children absorb, the more their excessive sanguine qualities are modified and the temperament harmonized.

In the case of melancholic children, who always tend to brood, the opposite treatment is needed. Sugar must be added to their food. Thus, we work right into the physical constitution of the liver, because the liver's basic activity differs according to the amount of sugar taken in. In effect, every outer activity penetrates deeply into the human organism.

A Waldorf school takes the greatest care that there is a close relationship between the teaching staff and the children's parents. Of course, a truly close relationship is possible to only a certain degree, since it depends on the degree of understanding on the part of the parents. We try our best, however, to encourage the parents to come to the teachers for advice about the most suitable diet for individual children. This is no less important than what is taught in the classroom.

We must not, however, think in a materialistic way that the body is responsible for everything. The body's role is to be a suitable instrument. We cannot teach a child to play the piano if that child's hands are incapable of working the keys; similarly, we cannot rid a child of melancholia if the child's liver is overactive, regardless of the psychological techniques of some abstract educational systems. But, if the liver's activity is regulated properly by sweetening the diet, such children will be able to use the physical body as a suitable instrument. Then—and not until then—psychological and spiritual techniques can be effective.

People frequently believe that education can be reformed by simply repeating abstract ideas. The whole world knows what education should be and how it ought to proceed. Yet true education requires an understanding of the human being that must be acquired gradually, and so I say that such ideas have no practical application (although I neither attack nor belittle the knowledge of nearly everyone on education). This sort of knowledge is like a person who wants a house that looks nice, is comfortable, and withstands the weather, and goes to someone who only knows about such qualities and thinks this is enough to build a house. But mere knowledge of these things has no practical value. This is just about all most people know about the art of education, and yet they think they can reform education. If I want a house built properly, I must go to an architect who knows in detail how a plan must be drawn, how the bricks must be laid, how massive the girders must be to bear the weight on them, and so on. Essentially, we must know in detail how human beings are constituted, and not speak vaguely about human nature in the abstract, as one might speak of a weatherproof, comfortable, and beautiful house.

The civilized world must realize that technique—a spiritualized technique, of course—is needed in every detail of the art of education. If this realization becomes widespread, it will be a real boon to all praiseworthy efforts toward educational reform today.

The significance of such principles is revealed most clearly when we consider children as unique individuals. At times, it has been the practice of schools not to allow the children who are unable to keep up with the work in one class to proceed to the next. In an art of education in which children are taught according to their age, there must gradually be no question of leaving a child behind in a class, since they will fall behind the sequence of teaching appropriate to their years. In Waldorf schools, of course, each class is made up of children of the same age. Thus, if children who should be in the fourth class are left behind in the third, the inner course of their education begins to conflict with their age. As much as possible, we avoid this in a Waldorf school. A child stays behind only in exceptional cases. We make every effort to handle individual children so that we do not need to hold them back.

For this, however, something else is certainly needed. As you know, there are children who do not develop properly and are in some way abnormal. At Waldorf schools, we have instituted a special needs class for those children. This class provides for children whose thinking, feeling, or volition are underdeveloped, and it has become very dear to our hearts. A child whom we cannot have in a class because of a weak soul force is placed in this separate class. And it is truly delightful to find a kind of competition among the teaching staff at the Waldorf school when we need to move a child from a normal class into the special needs class.

Given all I have said, you probably realize that there is real harmony among the Waldorf teaching staff, but there is always a certain struggle when such a thing has to be done. It means a real onslaught for Dr. Karl Schubert—a man so blessed in his ability for this work and to whom the special needs class had been entrusted. The teachers never like to give up a child to him. The children, too, feel it goes against the grain to leave their regular class and the teacher they love, and go into the special needs class. Nevertheless, it is a blessing that, before long, they do not want to leave the special needs class, because they have come to love Dr. Schubert. He is extremely well suited to teach this class because of his character and temperament and his infinite capacity for love. This capacity for love, devotion, and selflessness—which is the foundation of the art of teaching—is needed even more in an isolated class of this kind, which tries to bring children to a point where they can return to the right class for their age. This is the goal of the special needs class.

True knowledge of the human being shows us that it makes absolutely no sense to speak of the human spirit as abnormal or diseased, though of course when speaking colloquially in everyday life, there is no need to be fanatical and pedantic about it. Essentially, spirit and soul are never ill. Illness can occur only in the physical foundation and what thus enters the soul. Because we can approach the spirit and soul of earthly human beings through the body, when we treat "abnormal" children we must realize that the body's abnormality makes it impossible to approach the being of soul and spirit. As soon as we overcome a defect of the body or of body and soul in a child and are able to approach the nature of soul and spirit, we have done what is necessary. In this sense, therefore, our aim must always be to understand and recognize the delicate, intimate qualities and forces of the human body.

If we observe that a child does not understand in the normal way, that something prevents a connection with concepts and perceptions, we must conclude that there is some irregularity in the nervous system. Individual treatment helps—perhaps going more slowly in teaching, or stimulating the activity of will, and so on. For abnormal children, treatment must be individualized, and we do immeasurable good by using measures such as I have described. We must pay particular attention, of course, to physical education for such children.

For example, imagine a child for whom it is difficult to associate ideas mentally. We can accomplish much by giving physical exercises through which, out of the child's inner being, the whole organic system becomes more coordinated. For instance, we might tell a boy to touch the lobe of his left ear with the third finger of the right hand, asking him to do the exercise quickly. Then we may tell him to touch the top of his head with the little finger of the left hand, and then alternate these two exercises quickly. The organism is made to move in such a way that the child's thinking must flow swiftly into the movements. Thus, by stimulating the nervous system, it becomes a good foundation for the faculty needed when connecting or separating ideas and perceptions.

Truly wonderful experiences show us how children's spiritual nature can be stimulated by cultivating the physical body. Suppose, for example, a girl returns again and again to a single fixed idea. This tendency is obviously a great weakness in her soul. She simply cannot help repeating certain words or returning again and again to the same ideas. They grip her being and she cannot get rid of them. By observing such a child closely, we generally find that she walks too much on her heels and less with the toes and front part of the foot. Such a child must perform movements in which she pays attention to each step, repeating them until they eventually become habit. We will see extraordinary improvement in the inner soul defect of this child if it is not too late.[1] Indeed, much can be done in this way between seven and twelve. Nevertheless, we must understand how movements of, say, the right-hand fingers affect the speech organism, or how movements of the left-hand fingers affect the forces that arise from thinking and assist speech. We must understand, too, how toe-walking and heel-walking affect speaking and thinking, and especially volition. The art of eurythmy, working as it does with normal forces, teaches us a great deal when dealing with the abnormal. Eurythmy movements, which have an artistic quality when done by normal people, are modified to be therapeutic. Because the movements are derived from principles of the human organism itself, the faculties of spirit and soul—which can still be aroused during the period of growth—are given an impulse that arises from the physical body. This shows the necessity for understanding the unison between spirit, soul, and body when working with abnormal children in school.

The excellent course of teaching being developed by Dr. Schubert in this area of the Waldorf education is showing truly wonderful results. Of course, a great power of love and selflessness is needed whenever it is a matter of individualized treatment. These qualities are absolutely essential in the special needs class. And in many ways resignation is needed if one is to achieve any results at all, since one must work with what is there and can be brought out of the human being. If we attain only a quarter or a half of what would make the child normal,

---

1. Symptoms differ, of course, in each child. This is why true knowledge of the human being—one that can make individual distinctions—is so necessary. — R. STEINER

the parents are still not likely to be completely satisfied. But it is essential that any human action guided and directed by spirit should not depend on outer recognition; rather, one should become deeply aware of the sustaining power that grows from one's sense of inner responsibility. This power will gradually increase in an art of education that perceives, even in these intimate details of life, the harmony between the child's spirit, soul, and body. Understanding, perception, and observation are what teachers need above all; if teachers have these qualities, speech itself comes to life in their whole being. Instinctively and in an artistic way, such teachers bring to their teaching all that they have learned by observing the human being.

At a certain age, as I said yesterday, children must be led from plant and animal lore (which they understand more through their souls) to mineralogy, physics, and chemistry, which makes greater demands on their conceptual faculties and intellect, though it is very important that these subjects are not taught too early. During the phase of life when we convey the idea of causality to children, and when they learn of cause and effect in nature, it is essential to balance the inorganic, lifeless elements in nature study by leading them into art.

If we want to introduce art to children in the right way, not only must our teaching be artistic to begin with, but art itself must play a proper role in education. You can see that the creative arts are cultivated, if only from the fact that the writing lessons begin with a kind of painting. Thus, according to the Waldorf principle, we begin to give painting and drawing lessons at a very tender age. Modeling, too, is cultivated as much as possible, albeit only in a primitive way and after nine or ten. If, at the right age, children begin to model forms and figures, it has a wonderful vitalizing effect on their physical sight as well as the inner soul quality of sight. Most people go through life and never notice the most significant aspect of the objects and events of their environment. In fact, we have to learn how to do it before we can see in a way that gives us our true place in the world. If children are to learn to observe correctly, it is very good for them to begin, as early as possible, to model, bringing what they see with their head and eyes into the movements of their fingers and hands. Thus, we not only awaken their taste for the artistic qualities around them—say, in the arrangement of a room—and a dislike for the inartistic, but they also begin to observe the things in the world that should flow into human hearts and souls.

If we begin musical instruction with singing and lead gradually into instrumental playing, we develop the element of human volition. Musical instruction helps develop not only artistic qualities, but also purely human qualities, especially those of the heart and will. We must, of course, start with singing, but as soon as possible move toward an understanding of instrumental music, so that children can learn to distinguish the pure elements of music—rhythm, measure, and melody—from everything else, from imitative or pictorial qualities of music and so on. Increasingly, children must begin to realize and experience the purely musical element. By leading them into the area of art, building a bridge from play to life through art, between eleven and twelve—the proper time—we begin to teach them to understand art.

In the principles of education that form the goals of Waldorf teaching, it is vitally important for children to acquire some understanding of art at the right age. As a necessary balance, we must promote an understanding of art when children begin to realize that nature is ruled by abstract laws best understood through reason, and in physics they must learn the links between cause and effect. Children must realize how the various arts developed during different ages of human history, and how one or another motif in art plays a role in a particular era. This truly stimulates the elements needed for general development of the human being. In this way, too, we can develop qualities that are essential to moral instruction (as I will show tomorrow). If children understand art, human interrelationships will be quite different from what they would otherwise be. After all, what is the essence of understanding the world, my dear friends? It is the ability to reject, at the right moment, abstract concepts in favor of really understanding the world.

The mineral kingdom can be understood in terms of cause and effect. With the plant world, however, it is impossible to grasp everything through logic, reason, and intellect. The formative capacities of human beings must become involved, since concepts and ideas must become imagery. Any formative skills that we develop in children help them to understand the formations in plants. The animal kingdom can be comprehended only after the ideas for understanding it have been planted and developed in us through moral education. Only this activates the inner powers that enable us to understand the forces that form the animal structure from the invisible world. Few physiologists today understand the origin of an animal's form. In fact, the origin of the animal form arises from the structure of the organs that, in humans, become the organs of speaking and singing. That structure is the central origin of the forms and structure of animals. They do not reach the point of articulate speech; it reaches only the point of song as expressed by birds. In speaking and singing, formative forces radiate, shaping air waves and giving rise to sound. Life forces in the organs of speaking and singing pass back into the form of animals. It is impossible to understand the form of an animal unless we recognize that it develops musically, as it were, from organs that, at a higher level in human beings, become the organic structures related to music.

To understand the human being, we need an overall view of art, since the faculty of reason can comprehend only the inorganic aspects of our being. If, at the right moment, we know how to bring the faculty of mental representation over to artistic understanding, then and only then is it possible to truly understand the human being. Such understanding must be awakened by teaching art. If teachers possess real artistic feeling and can introduce children at the right age to Leonardo's *Last Supper* or Raphael's *Sistine Madonna*, showing not only the relationships between the various figures, but how color, inner perspective, and so on were treated in those days—in other words, if nature and history are both imbued with an inner quality of soul through teaching that conveys an understanding of art, then we bring the human element into all our teaching.

Nothing must be left undone in the way of imbuing children with an artistic feeling at the right age. Our civilization will not receive an impulse toward higher development until more art is introduced into the schools. Not only must teaching be permeated with the arts, but a living understanding of art, evoked by the teacher's own creativity, must be a balance to all the prosaic concepts of nature and history.

We consider this an essential part of Waldorf education. It is true—and every genuine artist feels this—that art is not a mere discovery of the human, but a domain that reveals the secrets of nature at a different level than that of ordinary intelligence. Art is a domain in which an artist gazes into the mysteries of the whole universe. Not until one sees the world itself as a work of art and nature herself as the artist are we ready to deepen our being in the religious sense. There is deep meaning in the words of a German poet: "Only through the dawn red of beauty can you enter the country of gnosis."[2] This is indeed true; when we grasp the whole human being through art, we also generate an understanding of the world in its totality. This is why our goal in teaching should be to add the purely human element to what prosaic culture requires. To this end, not only must teaching itself be full of artistic feeling, but an understanding of art must be awakened in the children. Only in this way can this end be achieved.

Art and science then lead to a moral and religious deepening—as we shall see tomorrow. But, as a preliminary to religious and moral progress, teaching must establish a balance: on one side of the scale are all those things that lead to prosaic life and bind us to the earth; on the other side are the balancing factors that lead to art. They enable us, in every moment of life, to raise what must first be worked out in the prose of life to an artistic level—and so lead directly into the spirit.

2. Friedrich Schiller (1759–1805), "Die Künstler" (1788): "Nur durch das Morgenrot des Schönen dringst du in der Erkenntnis Land."

EDUCATING TOWARD INNER FREEDOM

August 17, 1923

The fact that we have both boys and girls at the Waldorf school seems to serve two purposes. One is to shape the teaching according to the needs of the whole human being, since with either boys or girls alone, education always tends to become one-sided. The other is to work toward the kind of human interrelationship required especially by today's society, in which women have either gained their place in society or are trying to obtain it. The Waldorf art of education, therefore, deals with modern social struggles. Much that would remain remote from one gender or the other can thus be developed because boys and girls are educated together.

These lectures have shown that we attach great importance to the development of children's whole being—in spirit, soul, and body, and not just spirit and soul. This is why we engage the children in physical activity—especially activities that enable them to go into life with understanding. During the handwork lessons in the Waldorf school, you find boys and girls sitting together, all knitting and crocheting. This is absolutely natural, which is proved by the fact that the boys learn to knit and even darn socks with some pleasure. It never occurs to them that such work is inappropriate for men. We do not include such things just so the boys know how to do them, but for the sake of a general understanding of life. One of the main faults of present social conditions is that people have so little understanding of what others do. We must really stop isolating ourselves as individuals and groups and face one another with complete understanding. The main purpose of this kind of handwork is to teach practical skill in many different areas.

Though it may seem inconceivable, in my opinion no one can be a real philosopher who is unable to darn socks or mend one's clothes when needed. How can you have any intelligent concept of grand cosmic mysteries if you cannot even care for your own footwear? Can we really hope to enter cosmic mysteries, in a truly human sense, if we are incapable of dealing with the things right next to us? I realize that this may seem improbable, but I do believe that philosophers should have some understanding of how boots and such are made; otherwise, we simply adopt abstractions. This is an extreme example, perhaps, but I wanted to show that education must include both an ascent to the highest spiritual levels and descent into physical education and treatment.

From this kind of handwork, children can be guided to an ability to do manual work with intelligence and understanding. At the right age, which is relatively early, our children make their own toys and playthings. You have probably seen some on display here. They carve toys from wood, and thus we bring an element of art into their play. To lead play gradually into the creation of artistic forms, and then to the practical work, as just described, is completely in keeping with the needs of human nature. It is absorbing to find that the children's artistic sculptural activity turns naturally into making toys. Again, we lead from art as such into art as an aspect of industry. Children are shown how to make simple implements for use in the house, and at the same time learn to use saws, knives, and other cabinetmaking and carpentry tools. In addition to their regular lessons, both boys and girls love to be in our workshops, at work with a knife or a saw or other tools, and they are delighted when they succeed in making something useful. Thus, we stimulate all their instincts for the practical side of life. On the one hand, we develop a sense for practicality, and on the other, for the arts.

It is interesting to observe children when they learn something about the human organism—for example, the sculptural formation of skeleton or muscle formation. If they are given an artistic concept of the structure and functions of the human body, they begin to express, in a sculptural way, their ideas of the shape of some limb, not in a strict sense of imitation, but freely and creatively. Our children are allowed great freedom, even in their practical work, and they are allowed to follow their own sense of discovery. Their souls create wonderful forms once they learn to observe certain things in people or in animals with a truly artistic feeling for nature.

We teach this way, so that whatever children know, they know it with their whole being. Our culture is calculated to make us know everything with our heads. Facts rest in the head as though sitting on a couch; they rest in the head as though in bed; they are asleep, "meaning" only one thing or another. We carry them around, stored up in so many little compartments, which we otherwise prefer to leave alone. In the Waldorf school, the children do not merely "have an idea" in their heads; they feel the idea, since it flows into their whole life of feeling. Their souls live in the *sense* of the idea, which is not merely a concept but becomes a shaped form. The whole complex of ideas eventually becomes the human form, and finally passes into their volition. Children learn to transform what they think into action. When this happens, we do not find thoughts arising in any one part of the human being, with the will in another part nourished only by instinct. Such a person is really like a wasp. There are wasps that have a head, then a long stalk, and below this the rest of the body. Outwardly, it symbolizes not the modern human physical nature, but the nature of soul and spirit. One has a head, then a long stalk, and one's volition is an appendage to this. From the spiritual point of view, people today present a strange appearance—the head dangles in the air not knowing what to make of its own ideas.

This can be rectified by continually helping children to permeate their faculties of knowledge with feeling and volition. Modern systems of education have known for a long time that teaching has veered into one-sided intellectualism, that the head dangles in the air, and that a beginning must be made on the other side to develop practical skill and dexterity. But this does not really unite the two elements. Such a union is impossible unless knowledge of itself goes into practical skill, which is also permeated with the quality of thinking and inner understanding of the soul and spiritual participation.

Based on these principles, we can bridge the gap to moral and religious education. I already spoke of this and need only add that everything depends on giving all teaching and gymnastics in a form that makes children experience their physical nature as a revelation of spirit pouring willingly and creatively into their bodies. Children must never feel a separation between spirit and body. The moral and religious elements thus truly come to life in their feelings. The important thing to keep in mind is that, between the change of teeth and puberty, we must never indoctrinate morality and religion into children dogmatically, but by working on their feeling and perception according to this period of life. Children must learn to delight in goodness and to loathe evil, to love goodness and hate wickedness. In history lessons, the great historical figures and the impulses of various eras can be presented so that moral and religious sympathies and antipathies develop in the children. Thus we achieve something of supreme importance.

After puberty, around fifteen or sixteen, a change takes place in the children's inner nature, leading them from dependence on authority to their own sense of freedom and, hence, to the faculty of independent discernment and understanding. This must claim our closest attention in teaching. If we have awakened in children, before puberty, a feeling for good and evil and for what is divine or not, these feelings will arise from their own inner being afterward. Their understanding, intellect, insight, and power of discernment remain uninfluenced, and they form independent judgments out of their own being.

If we begin by telling children that they should do this or not do that, it stays with them throughout their life, and they will always think that such things are right or wrong. Convention will color everything. But those who have been educated properly will not stand within convention but use their own judgment, even regarding morality and religion, and this will develop naturally if it has not been engaged prematurely.

In a Waldorf school, children of fourteen or fifteen are allowed to find their own feet in life. We treat them as equals. They develop discernment, but look back to the authority that we represented and retain the affection they had for us when we were their teachers. Their power of discernment has not been limited if we have worked on their life of feeling properly. Therefore, once children reach fourteen or fifteen, we leave their soul nature and spirit free and, in the higher classes, appeal to their power of discernment and understanding. Such freedom in life cannot be achieved if we instill morality and religion in a dogmatic, canonical fashion. We must have worked solely on the children's powers of feeling and perception at the right age—between the change of teeth and puberty. The main thing is to enable young adults to find their place in the world with real confidence in their own powers of discernment. Thus, they will sense their real humanity, because their education has been completely human. Those who been unfortunate enough to have lost a leg or an arm are conscious of the damage. Children of fourteen or fifteen who have been educated according to modern methods begin to be aware of a sense of injury if they are not permeated with the qualities of moral judgment and religious feeling. Something seems to be missing in their being. There is no better heritage in the moral and religious sense than to raise children to regard the elements of morality and religion as an integral part of their being, so that they feel fully human because they are permeated with morality and warmed by religious feelings.

This can be achieved only when we work, at the proper age, only on the life of feeling and perception, and do not prematurely give the children intellectual concepts of religion and morality. If we do this before twelve to fourteen, we bring them up to be skeptics— men and women who later develop skepticism instead of healthy insight into the dogmas instilled in them—and not just skepticism in their thinking (the least important), but in feeling, which injures their feeling life. And, finally, there will be skepticism of volition, which brings moral error with it. The point is that our children will become skeptics if we present moral and religious ideals to them dogmatically; such ideals should come to them only through the life of feeling. Then, at the right age, they will awaken their own free religious and moral sense, which becomes part of their very being. They feel that only this can make them fully human. The real aim at Waldorf schools is to raise free human beings who can direct their own lives.

The Waldorf school is an organism complete and whole in itself. If one does not think of it this way, many of its educational principles may be misunderstood. People may think, for example, that if they visit the school two or three times and see what is done on those days, this is enough; they have seen how we teach. Of course, this is not the situation. People will see nothing of any significance in this way. What they see is like a fragment of a picture, from which they then form an opinion of the whole. Suppose you take a fragment of some great picture and show it to someone. How can you form an opinion of the whole from a fragment? The essential feature of Waldorf education is that every activity has its place in the school as a whole. People can understand a Waldorf school much better by studying the principles, its structure, and the living connection between the eighth class and the fourth class, for instance, or between the first and the tenth, instead of looking at an isolated fragment of the teaching. The organization of the school is conceived so that each activity has its place and time and fits into the whole. Individual subjects of instruction are introduced into the school from this perspective.

Here is a brief example how, in principle, eurythmy is given a place in the whole work. It is no good setting out to discover things that may then be introduced into the school activities. It is, as a rule, a wrong principle to invent things that are "good" for children—as happened too often in the Fröbel kindergarten system—and then make them an essential part of education.[1] Nothing should be introduced artificially to the school; everything should arise from life itself. Eurythmy was introduced to the Waldorf school not because we thought that children need gymnastic exercises, and thus set out to invent something. No, indeed! Eurythmy did not arise initially as an educational component at all. It came about around 1912 as the result of certain connections of destiny, but mainly as an art, not as an educational measure. We cannot understand eurythmy as applied in education if we think of it as a "educational" eurythmy, as opposed to eurythmy as an art. Consequently, I would have thought it better to give the eurythmy performances as an art here first, since that would have shown the underlying concept. Because eurythmy is an art, it is part of life, and this part of life has been put into a form that is suitable for educational purposes. Nobody can understand the eurythmy performed by children unless they realize what it will one day become as an art—and what it already is, perhaps more than many people think.

---

1. Friedrich Fröbel (1782–1852) created his kindergarten in 1837 to nurture self-direction, spontaneous play, and intimacy with nature in children. He taught that education should be creative and interactive, developing the whole personality in every aspect—social, moral, aesthetic, linguistic, spiritual, and scientific.

The Waldorf school began in 1919, and, because we found that eurythmy could be applied to educating children, we introduced it at the school. But this is secondary. This connection should be realized in everything else if we would understand the Waldorf school in relation to life. Teachers should have a free, unbiased view of life and be able to educate children for life. The more intimately teachers are connected with the life around them, the better it is for the school. Narrow-minded teachers who know nothing of life except the school itself can do little to develop the full humanity of their students. It is not a matter of a special method of teaching painting, for instance; if we want them to learn to paint, the principles of teaching should be drawn from the living art of painting, not from methods that have been invented especially for the purpose of education. The element of true art must be introduced into schools, not an intellectual substitute. And eurythmy makes it possible to again infuse art into human culture.

In addresses given before eurythmy performances, I explained the sense in which eurythmy is visible speech, expressed in movement. I just want to add something here about these figures, since this will further explain the relationship between eurythmy and art.[2] The idea for the figures originally came from Miss Maryon, but they have been made in forms that I think correct according to the principles of eurythmy.[3] Here (showing a figure), you have a picture of the sound "s." The figure does in a sense

---

2. These are figures carved from wood and painted in various colors. They represent the movements and gestures of eurythmy.
3. Louise Edith Maryon (1872–1924) helped Rudolf Steiner carve the large wooden sculpture, *The Representative of Humanity,* and helped design the "eurythmy houses" in Dornach, Switzerland.

represent a human being, but those who think in terms of today's conventional notions of a beautiful human form will not find much beauty in this figure. They will see nothing of what would seem beautiful in someone they met in the street. When making such figures, we may also have an eye for beauty of the human form, but the purpose is to represent the expression of eurythmy—the human

Steiner's sketch for a eurythmy figure "s"

being in movement. And so, in these figures, we have ignored anything that does not belong to the essence and form of movement itself, the feeling corresponding to a particular movement, and penetrating the basic character expressed by and coloring the movement. When you sing, you take into your whole organism—in a physical sense—the elements that move the soul. The movement occurs entirely within the bounds of the skin and remains invisible, flowing fully into the tone one hears.

The figure you see here (another figure) expresses music in movement. The soul's feeling is released from the human being, becomes spatial movement, and the artistic element is expressed as movement. We see what we otherwise only hear. Thus, these figures are intended only to suggest what a human being becomes while performing eurythmy, completely apart from any natural attributes. Each movement is indicated by the shape of the carving, and the wood is painted with a fundamental color. We have written on the back of these figures the names of the colors that correspond to the movements themselves and to the feeling inherent in the movements. The way eurythmists on a stage manipulate their veils becomes a continuation of the movement. Once eurythmists have learned to do this with skill, the veil will float freely, be withdrawn, caught up, or given a certain form at the right moment. The movement performed by the limbs is behind the feeling that is also expressed by manipulating the veil; the feeling is expressed in the floating veil. If a eurythmist has true feeling for the movement of arms or legs, the quality will naturally pass into the manipulation of the veil, and the feeling that should accompany movement in the veil will be felt.

When this movement (pointing to the figure) is being performed, the eurythmist must be able to sense that the arm is stretched out lightly in this direction, as though hovering in the air with no inner tension. In the other arm, a eurythmist must feel as though summoning all of one's muscular force and packing it tightly into the arm. One arm (the right) is held lightly upward; the left arm is tense, and the muscles almost throb. This is how the movement is given character, and this character makes an impression on the spectators. They can feel what the eurythmist is doing.

Now, when the people look at these figures, they may ask, where is the face and where the back of the head. But this has nothing to do with eurythmy. You will occasionally find those who are enthusiastic about the pretty face of a eurythmist, but I can assure you that this is not part of eurythmy. The face on this figure, which looks like it is turned to the left, is in fact facing you, and the color is used to emphasize the fact that the eurythmist should feel "eurythmic force" diffused lightly over the right side of the head, while the left side of the head is tense, imbued with inner strength. It is as though the head becomes asymmetrical—relaxed, as if "fluffed out," on the one side, and taut on the other.

The movements receive their true character in this way. The figures here express what should become visible in eurythmy. The same principles hold true of all artistic work. One should be able to look away from the substance, content, or prose, and enter the artistic element. A beautiful face on a eurythmist really corresponds to the prose quality. The eurythmist expresses the real beauty in eurythmy when the right side of the head is lightly diffused with eurythmic forces and the left side tense. So we can conceive that a plain face may be beautiful in the sense of eurythmy, and a beautiful face ugly.

In eurythmy, then, we have elements that are true of every art form, as all artists will agree. A great artist is not merely one who can paint a beautiful young face in a pleasing way. A true artist must be able to paint an old, wizened, wrinkled face in such a way that it becomes artistically beautiful. This must underlie all art.

I wanted to add these remarks about the eurythmy you have seen performed here. Let me just say that we introduced eurythmy into our Waldorf school because it affords such a wonderful contrast to ordinary gymnastics. As mentioned, physical exercises are carried out adequately in a Waldorf school, but regarding ordinary physical gymnastics, we elaborate them in such a way that, with every exercise, the children are first given a sense of spatial directions, which are, of course, fundamental. The children feel the directions of space, and then their arms follow it. In their gymnastics, they surrender to space. This is the only healthy basis for gymnastic exercises.

Space is conditioned in all directions. To an ordinary, abstract concept of space, there are three directions, which we cannot distinguish. They are present only in geometry. In fact, however, the head is above, the legs below, and this gives us above and below. Then we have right and left. We live in this direction of space when we stretch out our arms. The point is not to find some "absolute direction." Of course, we can turn this way or that. Then we have a forward and backward direction, front and back. All other directions of space are oriented in relation to these. If we understand space in this way, we can discover truly healthy movements for gymnastics, in which a person surrenders to the laws of space.

In eurythmy, the nature of a movement is determined by the human organism, and we can ask what the soul experiences in one movement or another. This is the principle behind the eurythmy movements for various sounds. What happens as one's forces flow into the limbs? In ordinary gymnastic exercises, we lend ourselves to space; in eurythmy we move in a way that expresses our being, according to the laws of our organism. The essence of eurythmy is to allow the inner to be expressed outwardly as movement. The essence of gymnastics is to fill the outer with the human being, so that one unites with the outer world.

To educate the whole human being, we can thus derive gymnastics from the polar opposite of eurythmy, in which the movements arise entirely from one's inner being. In any case, however, even when applied to education, the element of eurythmy itself must be derived from a true grasp of its artistic principles.

In my opinion, the best gymnastic teachers have learned from art. The impulses behind the gymnastics of

Greek schools and the Olympic Games were derived from art. And if the consequences of what I have said are fully realized, and all schoolwork is based primarily upon the element of art, we will also apply what I have described through the example of eurythmy to other areas of life and activity. We will not try to invent something for teaching, but imbue the school with real life. And then, out of the school, life will grow within society.

I have said that a school should be an organization in which each individual feature is an integral part of the whole. The threads of all the various activities necessary to the whole life of the Waldorf school are drawn together in the frequent teachers' meetings. Over the year, I myself am present at the majority of these meetings.[4] They are not held merely to prepare school reports, discuss administrative details, or talk about the punishments to be used when rules are broken. These meetings are really a living "higher education," since the college of teachers is a kind of permanent training academy. This is because the teachers' every practical experience in school becomes part of their own education. Teachers will always find something new for themselves and for the college of teachers if they educate themselves through their teaching, gaining a profound psychological insight into the practical side of education on the one hand, and on the other insights into the children's qualities, characters, and temperaments. All the experiences and knowledge acquired from the teaching are pooled at these meetings. Thus, in spirit and soul, the college of teachers becomes a whole, in which each member knows what the others are doing, what experience has taught them, and

4. For a record of those meetings, see *Faculty Meetings with Rudolf Steiner* (2 vols.), Anthroposophic Press, 1998.

what progress they have made as the result of their work in the classroom with the children. In effect, the college of teachers becomes a central organ from which the whole life of practical teaching flows, helping teachers to maintain their freshness and vitality. Perhaps the best effect of all is that the meetings enable teachers to maintain their inner vitality, instead of growing old in soul and spirit. It must be the teacher's constant aim to maintain a youthful freshness of soul and spirit, but this cannot be done unless real life flows through a central organ, just as human blood flows into and out of the heart. This is concentrated as a system of soul and spirit forces in the life that teachers work for in their meetings at the Waldorf school. Those meetings are held each week, and, as I said, sometimes I am present.

Now I want to mention something that seems trivial, but is important. As I said, we have boys and girls together in our classes. It naturally happens that, in some classes, girls are in the majority, in others the boys, and there are others in which the numbers are equal. A rationalist may visit these classes and spout all sorts of intellectual opinions, which nevertheless usually fail to hit the nail on the head regarding real life. If we teach in a class in which girls are in the majority, matters are not at all the same as in those classes where the number of boys and girls is the same, or where boys are in the majority. The classes are not given their individual character according to what the boys and girls do together—perhaps also the silly things they do together—but by intangible elements that wholly escape external, intellectual observation. Very interesting things come to light when we study this intangible life in the class. Of course, the teachers must not enter their classes and, stepping back with folded arms, "study" their students. If teachers bring enough vitality and devotion to their work, then, by simply taking the students with them in the right way in sleep, they wake up the next morning with significant discoveries about the previous day's events at school; they become aware of this process in a fairly short time, and all that should happen in this way will come about natually.

The very center and essence of the school are the teachers' meetings; likewise, at the periphery, the parents' evenings at the Waldorf school are extremely important. At least once a month—or regularly, anyway—we try to arrange evenings when the children's parents can gather and meet with the teachers, so that a link can be established with the children's home life. We think that the parents' understanding of their children's education is very important. Because we do not make up programs or schedules for our teaching but take it from life itself, we cannot adopt an attitude that claims to do the right thing, based on a schedule devised by some intelligent authority. We must come to sense what is right through our living interaction with the parents who sent their children to us. The echoes of these parents' evenings touch the teachers and give them what they need to maintain their own inner vitality.

Living beings do not live merely within their skin; nor do human beings exist only within the space of their skin. We always have a certain amount of air within us, and before we breathed in, it was outside and belonged to the atmosphere. And it is soon breathed out again. A living being belongs to the whole as a member of the universe, and our existence is unthinkable apart from it. And human beings are not isolated units in society, but integral members of it. We cannot live unless we are related to society just as intimately as our physical organism is related to the air and water that surrounds it. And, in this sense, it requires little to show how much depends on the school.

To illustrate such things, I generally try to use examples from ordinary life instead of something made up. Two days ago I entered a room here and observed a report from the Sunday school teachers. The first sentence refers to a speech at the yearly meeting of the Sunday School Union, given by a chairperson, an eminent man. He said that the Sunday schools had gradually isolated themselves from other religions in the world—that, in general, there is too little knowledge of religions. I read this on the bulletin board in the next room, and it is an important indication of what society needs for its inner vitalization today. I might as easily find the same sentiments elsewhere or in some leaflet handed out in the street. Everything tells the same story—that men and women today are not brought up with a broad view of life.

A broad view of life is essential to the Waldorf teachers, however, and they must communicate this to their students, so that education leads to broad interests in life. Everyone is so enclosed and confined today. Just consider professional training, which causes people to become almost ashamed of knowing anything beyond the pigeonhole of their own profession. We are always told to seek out experts or specialists, but the most important thing is to be bighearted. People should be able to participate with their hearts and souls in culture and society as a whole. This is what we attempt through the principles of education. First we imbue our teachers—in a Waldorf school, the first thing has been to educate the teachers—

and then the students through the teachers. The students are our great hope and goal; our purpose in every measure we adopt is that our students will carry its fruits into life in the right way.

That, my dear friends, is the attitude behind the art of education I have been describing. It is based fully on this principle. Our educational measures must arise from the human being, so that children develop fully in body, soul, and spirit, and as adults find their place in life, having grown, in body, soul, and spirit, within a religious, ethical, artistic, and intellectual life that enabled them to develop the virtues best suited to a life with other human beings. Essentially, every educational ideal must be based on this principle, and I am indeed grateful to those who made it possible for me to speak here on the subject.

I am sure you realized now that, although the principles of Waldorf education arose in one country, there is no question of any nationalism; rather, it is a matter of internationalism in the best sense, because it is a matter of the universal human. Our aim is to educate human beings with broad, rich interests—not men and women who belong to a particular class, nation, or profession. So I think you will agree that, although this art of education emanates from one country, it is permissible to speak of it in other lands, too.

It is an even greater pleasure to discover that, in connection with the subject of these lectures, a committee was formed to establish a school and bring Waldorf education to this country in a truly practical way.[5] When such schools are established today, we must create model schools as patterns, and this applies to Waldorf schools.

5. The New School, Streatham, London, now Michael Hall, Forest Row, Sussex.

This impulse cannot be truly fruitful until its principles are recognized by the broadest possible public opinion.

I recall that, in my early youth, I once saw in the comics a joke about architectural plans. (I mentioned something of the sort yesterday.) It said that one should not go to an architect, who would make all kinds of drawings and detailed calculations and then work to assemble the materials artistically. Rather, one should go to an ordinary mason who simply lays one brick upon another. This attitude still dominates the educational world. People tend to regard an architect's work as abstract, and they would like to see bricks laid upon bricks, with no concern about the principles behind the whole structure.

In any case, I am sincerely grateful to find such wonderful understanding and interest among you who have attended these lectures. First, let me thank Miss Beverley and her helpers; then our Waldorf teachers and other friends who have worked so hard and with such deep understanding; and also those who have added an artistic element to our conference. I am indeed grateful to all those whose interest and sincerity have brought this conference into being, which I hope will bear fruit through the new committee. As this interest spreads, we will be better able to serve the true principles of education. Your living cooperation demonstrates the fact that you have this at heart. I have given these lectures not only from the intellect, but also from a profound interest in the principles of true education.

And thus I would like to close these lectures with a parting greeting to you all.

THE THREE ERAS OF
HUMAN RELIGIOUS EDUCATION

August 12, 1923

Our weekday lectures are devoted to the subject of education. This Sunday lecture will be different. From the education of children on earth, the human art of education we are trying to develop, we look up to the "divine educators" of all humankind. Those great cosmic educators have guided us from age to age in history and evolution, through various religious and ethical aspirations related to the stages of our consciousness of the surrounding world. Despite the many valleys and lowlands that have interrupted the ascending development of humanity, when we look at history as one great whole, we see it as a continuous education of the human race, whereby divine consciousness repeatedly enters humanity.

In every era of human evolution, there has been some kind of initiation science, analogous in a way to what I outlined in *How to Know Higher Worlds*. There I described modern initiation, which leads from a mere knowledge of nature to knowledge of spirit. To initiation science, human evolution is revealed in a threefold light. We can look back to a very ancient era, which ended around the eighth century B.C. It was an era radiant with the light of the Mystery of Golgotha, when an eternal impulse entered human evolution through Jesus Christ. Today we are just beginning the third era, which we must deepen through a new initiation science.

Beyond what is given to humankind through the natural intelligence of reason, will, and feeling and through earthly education, each of these three eras has worked toward something else. In each era, humankind has sensed the existence of a grand mystery woven deeply into our destiny. It has assumed various forms, because the human race has passed through different conditions of soul during these eras. It is only in our modern age of abstractions that the human soul is thought to have remained more or less unchanged since humans first evolved (as is mistakenly imagined) from animals. A deeper science has enabled some to see without preconceptions into the reality of life, and they know that the human soul during the first era of evolution was nothing like it was during the era crowned by the Mystery of Golgotha. Nor was it the same as it is today, when we must work to understand the Mystery of Golgotha again if we do not wish to lose it as a fact of knowledge.

Therefore, let us consider the nature of the human soul in the ancient East, the age that gave us the wisdom of the Vedas and Vedanta. Everywhere today, people look back to the Vedas and Vedanta, often with great misunderstanding. If we look at the souls of those of the ancient East, even those souls living during the ancient Chaldean, Assyrian, Babylonian, and earliest Greek civilizations, we find that they were very different from souls today. The souls of those ancient times lived a more dreamlike, spiritual existence than do the souls of modern human beings, who while awake are fully surrendered to the senses, as well as their memory of sensory impressions and whatever the intellect can make of them. The real constitution of human souls today does not have the same form as those of the ancients. They had a much more instinctive wisdom of inner soul and spirit. What we might call a faculty of clear, conscious discernment today did not exist then. Ancient people experienced a weaving, mobile inner life, whose shadowy echoes remain in our dream life. It was an inner life, in which people knew with certainty that a soul—born of divine spirit before they were clothed in earthly form—weaved and moved through their bodies and lived within them.

In those times, people experienced their being in a kind of waking dream. They knew themselves as souls, and in this living inner experience, they experienced the body as a kind of sheath, a mere instrument for earthly life. Even while awake, they had this awareness of soul, though it was dreamlike. And they knew with clear conviction that, before a physical body clothed them on earth, they lived as souls in a divine spirit world. Direct inner perception revealed their soul and spirit, and, as a result, their awareness of death was very different from that of modern humankind.

Today people feel deeply connected with their bodies. Their inner awareness of soul is not detached from their physical life, as it was in earlier times. They see birth as a beginning, death as an end. The ancients' experience of the soul's eternal nature was so alive and intimate, however, that they felt lifted above birth and death in their contemplation of the soul's life. Birth and death were stages of growth and transformations of life. They knew the *reality* of a preearthly existence, and with equal certainty they knew that they would live beyond the gate of death. Birth and death were transitory occurrences in a continuous life.

Nevertheless, it has always been necessary for our immediate experience to be broadened and deepened by knowledge that penetrates the spirit world—an initiation science that tells us more than we find within ourselves or through earthly education. It fell to the old initiate teachers of ancient humanity to provide the answer to a certain mystery in the human soul. As I have said, the people of that time knew soul and spirit through direct experience. Yet for them, too, there was a great mystery in the soul: Through conception and birth, we enter physical life and walk the earth; we are clothed in a physical body made of the dead materials of outer nature; thus, we are enclosed in something foreign to our innermost being.

The great mystery before those of very ancient times, as they looked into their innermost being, was not a mystery of soul and spirit, but nature. It arose before them as they sensed the full inner reality of soul and spirit, and they felt a need to understand why they were clothed in a physical body so foreign to their true being. Initiation science—using the same forces that enabled them to gaze into the life of soul and spirit—had to teach them how to understand outer nature, whose manifestations are otherwise silent and unable to speak. The ancient teachers told them that, with enough training, one could come to understand outer nature if the forces that otherwise lead only to an inner knowledge of the soul were directed toward stones, plants, animals, clouds, stars, the courses of the sun and moon. One would see spirit not only within one's being, but also in a bubbling spring, in flowing rivers and mountains, in gathering clouds, in lightning and thunder, and in stones, plants, and animals.

Thus ancient initiation science spoke of looking into one's own being, experiencing soul and spirit, and finding the divine within. Initiation would train the power that sees the divine only in human beings, so that it could also see the divine in all of nature. Although clothed in an outer physical body, one could now know that body, too, is from God. Physical birth brings one into an earthly existence, which itself has a divine origin. Thus the purpose of ancient initiation science was to give humankind the sublime teaching that we can know, not only by looking inwardly, that we are born of God; we can see that the body, which enters the world through physical birth, is also born of God. Hence, all that initiation science teaches to the human soul can be expressed in three penetrating words: *Ex Deo nascimur.*

This was the first way that initiation wisdom worked on humanity and awakened an inner spiritual awareness. The ancient heathen cults became a form of animism, because people felt the need to justify their physical birth in nature. Nature was a soul mystery; in *Ex Deo nascimur* the mystery of nature was resolved, and people could feel their earthly existence sanctified, although when awake they still experienced themselves as beings of spirit and soul, transcending the physical.

As evolution proceeded, humanity's early, dreamy experience of soul and spirit, which was in fact a kind of innate knowledge of our real inner being, gradually faded into the background. We increasingly came to use the instruments of our physical body. In other words, the dreams of a soul and spirit life, which characterized human primal instinct, faded into darkness, and for the first time, during the millennium preceding the Mystery of Golgotha, people learned to use their outer senses and the intellect, which is connected with the senses. What we call "nature" appeared initially as an inner experience. It had been the task of the wise initiates to explain the spirit of nature to the human soul. The purely physical quality of outer nature was now presented as a mystery for the soul. Added to the ancient mystery of human earthly existence was another great mystery in the history of evolution: earthly death.

During the millennium before the Mystery of Golgotha, people came to regard earthly death with much greater intensity. Whereas in earlier times people had little sense of the body and a strong sense of soul and spirit, they now experienced their lives more fully in the physical body. Death, the enigmatic event connected with the physical body, was experienced as the greatest mystery of existence during this second era. The mystery of death emerged with great intensity among the ancient Egyptians, for example. They embalmed their dead, because they experienced a terror of death, since they saw the relationship between death and the physical body, in which they sensed their own existence. The first mystery had been a question of how to live in one's earthly body. The second was a question of how to go through earthly death.

When human beings still gazed up to the soul and spirit, which were experienced directly by instinctive clairvoyance, they knew that, once the chains of earthly existence fall away, they would no longer belong to the earth. The earthly being would change, and they would again live in realms beyond earth and be united with the stars. For in their instinctive life, the soul knew the stars in spirit; people could read their destiny in the stars and feel united with the sun and moon. They knew that they came from the spirit in the stars, and that they would return to the stars after earthly death. But now this all became a mystery. One confronted death and saw it as

the body's end. One's soul was felt to be inwardly bound
to the body, and with a deep awareness of this mystery, a
question arose: What happens to me when I die? How do
I go through the gate of death? At first, there was nothing
on the earth that answered these questions.

The ancient initiates could explain the mystery of
nature. They taught, *"Ex Deo nascimur,"* if we translate
their words into a later language. Awareness of pre-
earthly existence, to which human beings return after
death, had been so clear in earlier times, but it came to be
hidden from the human soul. The instinctive knowledge
that one's soul and spirit reached up to the stars was no
longer available. And then a powerful event occurred.
The spirit of the world of stars, whom a later age called
Christ, and the earlier Greeks called *Logos,* descended to
earth as a spiritual being and assumed the human body
of Jesus of Nazareth. It was humanity's destiny to experience the greatest event of all earthly existence. He whose
life had been divined by the ancients as they looked to the
stars, the Godhead of whom the divine on earth is also
part, passed through earthly life and death. The death
and resurrection of Christ were the most essential thing
for early Christians who truly understood Christianity.

God, who in earlier times revealed himself only from
the stars, passed through a human body and carried the
solution of the second mystery of existence, the mystery
of death, inasmuch as the mystery was revealed in the so-
called gnosis by initiates at the time of the Mystery of
Golgotha. The initiates could teach that the being who
had lived in eternity among the stars had now descended
into a human body and vanquished earthly death. Christ
had become an "extract" of the cosmic spirit, *Logos.* The
ancient initiates pointed to nature and taught that nature

is born of God. Now, initiates could teach how human beings can be united with the divine being who descended into Jesus of Nazareth and then passed, as all must, through the gate of death. But he conquered death. It was possible for people to solve the second mystery, that of Death, as they had solved the mystery of nature.

Buddhism tells us that the Buddha discovered the Four Noble Truths, one of which awoke within him at the sight of a corpse, and he was seized by the utter desolation of the human body in death. About six centuries before the Mystery of Golgotha, as a last remnant of ancient thinking, the Buddha had the vision of death. Six hundred years after the Mystery of Golgotha, people began to look at a dead human form on the Cross. Just as the Buddha believed that the corpse revealed to him, as a final fragment of ancient wisdom, the great truth of death, now those imbued with the Christ impulse observed a dead figure on the Cross, the crucifix, and in that figure experienced a heavenly guarantee of life beyond death; for death had been conquered by Christ in the body of Jesus.

Because they feared death, the Egyptians embalmed their bodies to "save" human nature forces from death. This was in the age of *Ex Deo nascimur*. The early Christians in whom the impulse of esoteric Christianity continued to live buried their dead, holding services over the grave with the conviction that death had been conquered by the soul united with Christ. This certainty flowed from the Mystery of Golgotha, and the tomb became an altar. Thus, God the Father was the answer to the mystery of nature. Christ was the answer to the mystery of death. Death had lost its sting. Through an argument more powerful than had ever been necessary, death became a metamorphosis of life.

Gnosis (which was later exterminated, leaving only fragments) shows that Christian initiates contemplated the Mystery of Golgotha with the certainty that Christ had descended to earth to bring new life to the deathly forces of earth. They were able to instill into humanity the truth about the union of mortal human beings on earth with Christ. Through Christ, we redeem the forces of death within us and awaken them to life. Thus those initiates were able to impart a new awareness of immortality to humankind: Souls can be united with the one who experienced the Mystery of Golgotha. We can live in Christ's life, death, and resurrection. If one's earthly life is more than a mere natural phenomenon, if Christ's kingdom is awakened in one's interactions with others, then one lives in communion with Christ. The divine Christ becomes your brother; both in death and in life, you die in Christ. The truth of life in God the Son, or Christ, could now be added to the primeval truth of our birth from God the Father: *Ex Deo nascimur, in Christo Morimur,* or *In Christ we die, as souls we live.* This was the nature of human wisdom during the era beginning a millennium before the Mystery of Golgotha and ending around the end of the fifteenth century. We are now in the third era, which we must come to understand. In the education of humankind as directed by the great, divine world teachers, the truth *In Christ the Son we die* was added to *From God the Father we are born.*

As we look back at ancient history, we see clearly the great mysteries of the first and second eras. The mystery of the third era, which began several centuries ago, is still relatively unknown and little felt, though it is present to our subconscious feelings, and we yearn for its resolution as deeply as we once yearned for a resolution of the mystery of our physical nature and bodily death.

Since the fourteenth and fifteenth centuries, humanity has gained knowledge that goes deeply into nature. Just consider the starry heavens, which were once revealed in dream consciousness, in which the ancients saw their destiny. External calculations, geometry, and mechanics have taught us much more about the stars since the beginning of our present age. The science of the stars, biology, and botany have spread as purely natural sciences. It was very different in the first era of human evolution, and again in the second, when people knew deep in their souls the reality of the divine, which the old clairvoyant soul powers read in the stars, and which in Christ descended into the body of Jesus of Nazareth. Christ was alive among humankind. The people of the second era looked to the Christ, they felt him in their hearts, and in this deep communion they experienced revelations of the cosmic spirit, which had once been revealed to ancient dreamy clairvoyant consciousness and purpose and meaning to earthly life. During that second era, people lived in cosmic spheres, insofar as they lived in communion with Christ, who had descended to earth from those cosmic spheres.

Then came the third era, when the world of stars was understood merely in terms of calculation. People looked through telescopes and spectroscopes and discovered in the stars the same dead elements and substances that exist on earth. During this era, people no longer see Christ as the being who came down from the stars, because they do not understand the stars themselves as an expression of the spirit as it weaves in the cosmos. For humanity today, there is no God or Christ in the cosmos.

Thus it is that our inner consciousness is in danger of losing Christ, and the first signs are already visible. The ideas of divine wisdom, or theology, which for centuries knew of the Christ revelation, are in many respects today powerless to find Christ the God in the human Jesus of Nazareth. Many who contemplate the age of the Mystery of Golgotha no longer find Christ as a cosmic being; they find only the man, Jesus of Nazareth. God is absent from the starry heavens, which are now merely a part of nature. People no longer recognize the one who passed through the Mystery of Golgotha as the being whose physical kingdom is the entire cosmos, yet also entered the human Jesus of Nazareth. To the degree that these things are deeply experienced inwardly, there is a difference between those who walk the path of modern initiation and those who merely study natural science. This science has lost the cosmic spirit, and a danger approaches that humanity will also lose the Christ, even in Jesus of Nazareth.

Therefore, those today who go more deeply into the natural sciences, which have blossomed during this third period of human evolution (since the fourteenth or fifteenth century) feel the third great mystery of earthly development. They look back in history to the first great mystery, that of our earthly nature, and to the second mystery, earthly death. Thus, the third mystery arises from within, whispering something that people do not want to face yet, though they feel it subconsciously in their hearts.

Modern initiates can confirm that our world once spoke to human beings as cosmic spirit; that in ancient times, people were awake to the cosmos, but that cosmic consciousness and the sense of oneness with the Christ, who descended to earth to preserve awareness of cosmic spirit, faded away. Now we live in a cosmos that reveals itself only externally. Modern cosmology is like a dream. It observes the cosmos through telescopes, measuring and weighing it. This is today's dream. Instead of uniting us with cosmic spirit, this dream separates us from him.

Thus, the third great mystery, the cognitive sleep of humankind, confronts people of the third era of evolution, not just the "uninitiated," but also initiation science. The deepest thinkers have sensed this. Descartes felt it, and he finally began to doubt all knowledge arising from outer nature. Initially, this was felt only vaguely. People must increasingly come to understand that all of the accumulated knowledge of the past five centuries is really a sleeping existence. This third great mystery must gradually become clear to us. In previous times, people wondered why they had to live in a physical body and why they had to die. In the third era, new questions arise in our hearts: Why is our cognitive sleep directed only toward outer nature? How can we awake from this dream that can only measure the universe? How can we move beyond the cosmos of astrophysicists and chemists and face a cosmos that, in the depths of our being, reunites us with its essence? How can we awake from dreaming cognition?

Ex Deo nascimur. This was the answer from initiates when humankind first asked why people live in an earthly body. During the age of the Golgotha Mystery, initiates tried to answer the question of death by connecting humankind with Jesus Christ, who had passed through death: *In Christo morimur.* And in our age and in the coming centuries, it is the task of initiation science to lead humankind gradually to divine awareness, making it possible for people to become inwardly awake to spiritual knowledge of the cosmos. Today's initiation science that must arise through *Anthroposophia* is not intended to be a mere extension of the present cognitive sleep, although people are proud of their present knowledge and its wonderful results. Anthroposophic initiation awakens this cognitive sleep; it would awaken humanity, which is bound by the dreams of reason and intellect.

Hence, the initiation science born of *Anthroposophia* is not a mere extension of information and discoveries, but an impulse to awake. Its purpose is to show us how to awake from our sleep of life. Thus, just as the earliest initiates explained *Ex Deo nascimur,* and those who came later *In Christo morimur,* this new initiation wisdom bears a future life of conscious spiritual knowledge, leading to a deepening of religious feeling and to a divine consciousness. This initiation wisdom leads to cognition of the Christ, the *Logos,* who passed through the Mystery of Golgotha and weaves and works through the cosmos. Inasmuch as we will gradually grow to awareness of our cosmic existence, the initiation science intended to bring a Christology in the truest sense (and an art of education in a narrower sense) strives to bring a religious feeling into the practical life it wishes to serve.

Out of God we are born as physical human beings. In Christ we die—that is, as souls, we live. Initiation science strives to add to this the third truth: When we work through the new initiation toward spirit, then, even in earthly life, we come to life in the spirit. We experience an awakening of knowledge, whereby all of life is bathed in the light of true religion and moral goodness arising from inner devotion. In other words, this new initiation science tries to supplement the answers to the first and second mysteries of initiation as expressed by *Ex Deo nascimur* and *In Christo morimur,* while also answering them anew and restoring them to human souls. It endeavors to bring this truth in a fresh and clear way to human hearts. This truth will awaken spirit in human hearts and souls: in the understanding of the living spirit, we ourselves, in body, soul, and spirit, shall reawaken: *Per spiritum sanctum reviviscimus.*

CLOSING ADDRESS

August 17, 1923

I have already expressed my gratitude to the committee, to Miss Beverley, and to all of you who have devoted the past two weeks to studying our subject. Rest assured that a warm sense of gratitude will remain with me as a pleasant memory of this lecture course. Now, I just want to add a few words to the perspectives expressed in the lectures. Most of you are familiar with the relationship between Waldorf educational principles and spiritual science as it exists in the anthroposophic movement, and perhaps as we close this conference you will allow me to say a few words on this subject.

People today still have an erroneous view of the anthroposophic movement, perhaps because one of my wishes—however impractical—cannot be fulfilled. It is true that the Waldorf movement grew out of the anthroposophic movement, but it is equally true that I would truly prefer to give a different name to that movement every week. I realize that it would be terribly confusing, but I would very much like to do this, because names actually do a great deal of harm today. The confusion this would create in people's minds is obvious—if letterheads were changed each week, and people were to receive a letter printed with the previous week's name, "since superseded." Nevertheless, it would be very good for the anthroposophic movement if it had no permanent name, because most people today are concerned only with names and never get to the subject itself.

People can turn to a Greek lexicon and, in their own language, invent words to express *anthroposophy*, and thus invent an idea of what spiritual science is and judge us accordingly. People form an opinion about us according to their idea of the name, thus avoiding the trouble of looking into the substance of spiritual science.

The book table at the door of this hall has disappeared, but I assure you that I shuddered every day as I arrived and saw the mass of literature there. I would be happy if there were less of it, but people must study spiritual science, of course—there is that. One cannot look only a name, and this is why it would be such a good thing if we were spared the need to have one. Obviously, that would not work, but in a lecture course about applying spiritual science to life, I think it shows how far we are from any sectarianism or any desire to fill people's heads with dogma. The only goal of spiritual science is to acquire knowledge of the essence of cosmic truths. And if there is any wish to participate constructively in evolution, it is essential to truly understand the world's events.

It is sad that there is so little inclination to look into the course of world events today, but this is in fact the purpose of spiritual science. This, too, is why we can speak of special areas such as education without beginning with a scheduled program or the like. In establishing the Waldorf school, we saw that it is not a matter of introducing the rigid dogma that spiritual science is believed to represent; rather, we never introduce anything of spiritual science as it is intended for adults. We realized that spiritual science must live within us as a power that leads to a fresh understanding of human nature and an unbiased observation of the world, which in turn leads to free activity.

Not long ago, I read an extraordinary criticism; it was very antagonistic. There are many such criticisms, and I have no wish to discuss them in detail. This particular critic said that I seem to make efforts to be unbiased—but the words implied a serious criticism. I would have thought it was a common duty today—especially in spiritual matters—to work toward open-minded knowledge, but apparently it can be a matter for severe reproach. Nevertheless, I think that the subject of education in particular can lead to ready understanding between the Continent and England, and when I see what your attitude has been toward these lectures, I consider it as a very good sign. When trying to describe our time, people like to use the abstract phrase, "We are living in an age of transition." Of course, every age is an age of transition—always from one period to the next. The point is, however, what is it that is in transition? At the present time, all kinds of signs indicate that we are indeed caught up in the process of a grand transition.

Perhaps the best way to explain this is to lead your thoughts back to the stage of spiritual evolution reached in England during the twelfth to the fourteenth centuries. At the beginning of the fourteenth century, those who claimed to be cultured spoke French. English consisted of dialects that did not enter the general culture of the people, and the language of science was Latin. If, for example, we want to study the general nature of education in England during the fourteenth century, around 1364, we can do so from Higden's *Polychronycon*, which was published at the time.[1] Written in Latin, the book makes it

1. The lecture notes give the name incorrectly as "Hykte." In 1385, John Trevisa translated the text into English. See Ranulf Higden, *The Polycronycon: A Medieval Universal History*, London: J Barrett, 1992. — ED.

clear that the medium of culture was Latin. When that book was written, the language of culture was Latin, but schools were being established in which the national language was finding its way into education (and this was also true of other countries in Europe). Schools were established in Winchester and Oxford, in which the national tongue was already in use. In the late fourteenth century, we find the important transition from Latin—an international language—to the national tongue.

Similar transitions occurred earlier or later in other regions of the civilized world, and this phenomenon has great significance. Insofar as England is concerned, we can place it in the late fourteenth century. When Higden wrote his book in 1364, he was able to tell us that the Latin tongue was still the universal medium for education. When a certain Trevisa translated it into English in 1385, we are told that English had been introduced into schools. Thus, we see the transition from the international language of Latin, which cultured people all over the world used to discuss matters of education, to the age when national language rises above the level of dialect to become, for various peoples, the medium for education. This is a significant transition.

According to the anthroposophic view, we can describe it as a transition from the age of the *intellectual soul*, in which people felt more connected to the universe, to that of the *spiritual soul*, in which human beings are to become aware of their free inner power of resolve and action. This transition is the essence of modern civilization; this alone could institute the great cosmic process in which we are still immersed today.

The effects of this emerging national language did not enter human souls and hearts immediately. Initially, in

England, too, the Renaissance movement, or "Humanist" movement, began to flow north from the south. In its early days, the Humanist movement indeed aspired to the qualities of the spiritual soul, but never reached the point of real understanding. Thus, it was established that, to be truly human, one must absorb the humanist, classical culture. This struggle for human freedom and the exercise of inner, spiritual activity has continued for centuries, right up to our own day. But increasingly, the needs of civilized humanity become obvious.

In the age before this urge toward spiritual soul, language itself gave rise to the element of internationalism, making it possible for the cultured people of every country to work with one another. Language was the international element. We can place the actual transition in the second half of the fourteenth century, when this language could no longer serve as a medium for international understanding. There was an urge within human beings to develop spiritual activity from depths of their own being, and they resorted to national language, which made it increasingly necessary to understand at a level higher than that of language or speech.

We need spirituality that no longer arises from mere language, but issues more directly from the soul. A true realization of spiritual science that connects history with the present time shows that its purpose is to find, throughout the world, an international medium of understanding, through which people can find their way to one another—one that transcends the level of language.

All interaction between human beings is incorporated by the faculty of speech into sounds communicated through the air. In speech, our being is truly active in the material world. If we understand one another at a level beyond speech by means of deeper elements in the soul—through thoughts carried by feeling and warmed by the heart—then we have an international medium of understanding, but we need heart for it to come into being. We must find the path to human spirit at a level beyond speech. The search for a language of thought—and everything related to philosophy, education, religion, and art—is the purpose of the anthroposophic movement during the present period of history.

Ordinary speech lives and moves through the medium of air and exists in the material world. The language that spiritual science looks for will move through the pure element of light passing from soul to soul and heart to heart—and this is not just a figure of speech. Modern civilization will need such a medium of understanding, not just for the matters of high culture, but also for everyday life. Before this can be realized, of course, many different kinds of conferences will be held, but during recent times, the fruitfulness of such congresses for healing human beings has not been very apparent. The anthroposophic movement would like to intercede for a true healing of humankind, which can arise only through mutual understanding. Because of this, we try to understand our own age within the context of history, so that we can become human in the true sense—human beings with a fully aware soul, as was true of another stage of evolution, when Latin was the medium of international understanding. The function once served by Latin must now be taken up by universal human ideas, through which we can find our way to other people all over the earth.

Anything that lives in the world requires soul and spirit as well as a physical body. In the very truest sense, spiritual science would be the soul and spirit of the "body" as it has entered our global civilization as the world economy and the other worldly activities. Spiritual science does not disdain or avoid the most practical areas of life; it would gladly infuse them with the only element that can lead to real progress in human evolution.

I am so infinitely grateful that you wish to understand how, in this sense, our educational attempts are based on the anthroposophic movement as a true expression of the present stage of evolution. I am grateful, too, for your interest in the illuminations and shades of meaning I have tried to introduce, in addition to speaking of the historical significance of the aims of this art of education. And I especially thank you for your cordial feelings toward a course of lectures given with the object of describing the goals of Waldorf education toward the progress of civilization as it confronts today's needs.

I have tried to describe how Waldorf education points to the deepest needs of humankind in the present age, and, as I say, your sympathetic understanding will indeed remain in my heart and soul as a very good memory of this course.

THE FOUNDATIONS
OF WALDORF EDUCATION

THE FIRST FREE WALDORF SCHOOL opened in Stuttgart, Germany, in September 1919, under the auspices of Emil Molt, director of the Waldorf Astoria Cigarette Company and a student of Rudolf Steiner's spiritual science and particularly of Steiner's call for social renewal.

It was only the previous year—amid the social chaos following the end of World War I—that Emil Molt, responding to Steiner's prognosis that truly human change would not be possible unless a sufficient number of people received an education that developed the whole human being, decided to create a school for his workers' children. Conversations with the minister of education and with Rudolf Steiner, in early 1919, then led rapidly to the forming of the first school.

Since that time, more than six hundred schools have opened around the globe—from Italy, France, Portugal, Spain, Holland, Belgium, Britain, Norway, Finland, and Sweden to Russia, Georgia, Poland, Hungary, Romania, Israel, South Africa, Australia, Brazil, Chile, Peru, Argentina, Japan, and others—making the Waldorf school movement the largest independent school movement in the world. The United States, Canada, and Mexico alone now have more than 120 schools.

Although each Waldorf school is independent, and although there is a healthy oral tradition going back to the first Waldorf teachers and to Steiner himself, as well as a growing body of secondary literature, the true foundations of the Waldorf method and spirit remain the many lectures that Rudolf Steiner gave on the subject. For five years (1919–1924), Steiner, while simultaneously working on many other fronts, tirelessly dedicated himself to the dissemination of the idea of Waldorf education. He gave manifold lectures to teachers, parents, the general public, and even the children themselves. New schools were established, and the movement grew.

Whereas many of Rudolf Steiner's foundational lectures have been translated and published in the past, some had never appeared in English, with many virtually unobtainable. To remedy this situation and to establish a coherent basis for Waldorf education, Anthroposophic Press (now SteinerBooks) decided to publish the complete series of Steiner's lectures and writings on education in a uniform series. This series constitutes an authoritative foundation for work in educational renewal for Waldorf teachers, parents, and all educators.

Rudolf Steiner's Works on Education

I. *Allgemeine Menschenkunde als Grundlage der Pädagogik: Pädagogischer Grundkurs*, 14 lectures, Stuttgart, 1919 (GA 293). Previously *Study of Man*. **The Foundations of Human Experience** (Anthroposophic Press, 1996).

II. *Erziehungskunst Methodische-Didaktisches*, 14 lectures, Stuttgart, 1919 (GA 294). **Practical Advice to Teachers** (Rudolf Steiner Press, 1988).

III. *Erziehungskunst*, 15 discussions, Stuttgart, 1919 (GA 295). **Discussions with Teachers** (Anthroposophic Press, 1997).

IV. *Die Erziehungsfrage als soziale Frage*, 6 lectures, Dornach, 1919 (GA 296). Previously *Education as a Social Problem*. **Education as a Force for Social Change** (Anthroposophic Press, 1997).

V. *Die Waldorf Schule und ihr Geist*, 6 lectures, Stuttgart and Basel, 1919 (GA 297). **The Spirit of the Waldorf School** (Anthroposophic Press, 1995).

VI. *Rudolf Steiner in der Waldorfschule, Vorträge und Ansprachen*, 24 lectures and conversations and one essay, Stuttgart, 1919–1924 (GA 298). **Rudolf Steiner in the Waldorf School: Lectures and Conversations** (Anthroposophic Press, 1996).

VII. *Geisteswissenschaftliche Sprachbetrachtungen*, 6 lectures, Stuttgart, 1919 (GA 299). **The Genius of Language** (Anthroposophic Press, 1995).

VIII. *Konferenzen mit den Lehrern der Freien Waldorfschule 1919–1924*, 3 volumes (GA 300a–c). **Faculty Meetings with Rudolf Steiner**, 2 volumes (Anthroposophic Press, 1998).

IX. *Die Erneuerung der pädagogisch-didaktischen Kunst durch Geisteswissenschaft*, 14 lectures, Basel, 1920 (GA 301). **The Renewal of Education** (Anthroposophic Press, 2001).

X. *Menschenerkenntnis und Unterrichtsgestaltung*, 8 lectures, Stuttgart, 1921 (GA 302). Previously *The Supplementary Course:*

Upper School and *Waldorf Education for Adolescence.* **Education for Adolescents** (Anthroposophic Press, 1996).

XI. *Erziehung und Unterricht aus Menschenerkenntnis,* 9 lectures, Stuttgart, 1920, 1922, 1923 (GA 302a). The first four lectures are in **Balance in Teaching** (Mercury Press, 1982); last three lectures in **Deeper Insights into Education** (Anthroposophic Press, 1988).

XII. *Die gesunde Entwicklung des Menschenwesens,* 16 lectures, Dornach, 1921–22 (GA 303). **Soul Economy: Body, Soul, and Spirit in Waldorf Education** (Anthroposophic Press, 2003).

XIII. *Erziehungs- und Unterrichtsmethoden auf anthroposophischer Grundlage,* 9 public lectures, various cities, 1921–22 (GA 304). **Waldorf Education and Anthroposophy 1** (Anthroposophic Press, 1995).

XIV. *Anthroposophische Menschenkunde und Pädagogik,* 9 public lectures, various cities, 1923–24 (GA 304a). **Waldorf Education and Anthroposophy 2** (Anthroposophic Press, 1996).

XV. *Die geistig-seelischen Grundkräfte der Erziehungskunst,* 12 Lectures, 1 special lecture, Oxford, 1922 (GA 305). **The Spiritual Ground of Education** (Anthroposophic Press, 2004).

XVI. *Die pädagogische Praxis vom Gesichtspunkte geisteswissenschaftlicher Menschenerkenntnis,* 8 lectures, Dornach, 1923 (GA 306). **The Child's Changing Consciousness as the Basis of Pedagogical Practice** (Anthroposophic Press, 1996).

XVII. *Gegenwärtiges Geistesleben und Erziehung,* 14 lectures, Ilkeley, 1923 (GA 307). **A Modern Art of Education** (Anthroposophic Press, 2004) and **Education and Modern Spiritual Life** (Garber Publications, 1989).

XVIII. *Die Methodik des Lehrens und die Lebensbedingungen des Erziehens,* 5 lectures, Stuttgart, 1924 (GA 308). **The Essentials of Education** (Anthroposophic Press, 1997).

XIX. *Anthroposophische Pädagogik und ihre Voraussetzungen,* 5 lectures, Bern, 1924 (GA 309). **The Roots of Education** (Anthroposophic Press, 1997).

XX. *Der pädagogische Wert der Menschenerkenntnis und der Kulturwert der Pädagogik,* 10 public lectures, Arnheim, 1924 (GA 310). *Human Values in Education* (Rudolf Steiner Press, 1971).

XXI. *Die Kunst des Erziehens aus dem Erfassen der Menschenwesenheit,* 7 lectures, Torquay, 1924 (GA 311). *The Kingdom of Childhood* (Anthroposophic Press, 1995).

XXII. *Geisteswissenschaftliche Impulse zur Entwicklung der Physik. Erster naturwissenschaftliche Kurs: Licht, Farbe, Ton—Masse, Elektrizität, Magnetismus,* 10 lectures, Stuttgart, 1919–20 (GA 320). *The Light Course* (Anthroposophic Press, 2001).

XXIII. *Geisteswissenschaftliche Impulse zur Entwicklung der Physik. Zweiter naturwissenschaftliche Kurs: die Wärme auf der Grenze positiver und negativer Materialität,* 14 lectures, Stuttgart, 1920 (GA 321). *The Warmth Course* (Mercury Press, 1988).

XXIV. *Das Verhältnis der verschiedenen naturwissenschaftlichen Gebiete zur Astronomie. Dritter naturwissenschaftliche Kurs: Himmelskunde in Beziehung zum Menschen und zur Menschenkunde,* 18 lectures, Stuttgart, 1921 (GA 323). Available in typescript only as **"The Relation of the Diverse Branches of Natural Science to Astronomy."**

XXV. *The Education of the Child and Early Lectures on Education* (a collection; Anthroposophic Press, 1996).

XXVI. Miscellaneous.

FURTHER READING
ON EDUCATION & ANTHROPOSOPHY

By Rudolf Steiner:

Anthroposophical Leading Thoughts: Anthroposophy As a Path of Knowledge, The Michael Mystery, London: Rudolf Steiner Press, 1998 (GA 26).

At Home in the Universe: Exploring Our Suprasensory Nature, Great Barrington, MA: Anthroposophic Press, 2000 (GA 231).

Autobiography: Chapters in the Course of My Life, 1861–1907, Great Barrington, MA: Anthroposophic Press, 1999 (GA 28).

Christianity as Mystical Fact, Great Barrington, MA: Anthroposophic Press, 1996 (GA 8).

Founding a Science of the Spirit, London: Rudolf Steiner Press, 1999 (GA 95).

From the History & Contents of the First Section of the Esoteric School, 1904–1914, Great Barrington, MA: Anthroposophic Press, 1998 (GA 264).

How to Know Higher Worlds: A Modern Path of Initiation, Great Barrington, MA: Anthroposophic Press, 1994 (GA 10).

Intuitive Thinking As a Spiritual Path: A Philosophy of Freedom, Great Barrington, MA: Anthroposophic Press, 1995 (GA 4).

Nature's Open Secret: Introductions to Goethe's Scientific Writings, Great Barrington, MA: Anthroposophic Press, 2000 (GA 1).

An Outline of Esoteric Science, Great Barrington, MA: Anthroposophic Press, 1998 (GA 13).

The Spiritual Guidance of the Individual and Humanity, Great Barrington, MA: Anthroposophic Press, 1991 (GA 15).

Theosophy: An Introduction to the Spiritual Processes in Human Life and in the Cosmos, Great Barrington, MA: Anthroposophic Press, 1994 (GA 9).

A Way of Self-Knowledge, Great Barrington, MA: Anthroposophic Press, 1999 (GA 16, 17).

What Is Anthroposophy? Great Barrington, MA: SteinerBooks, 2002.

What Is Waldorf Education? Three Lectures, Great Barrington, MA: SteinerBooks, 2003.

By Other Authors:

Aeppli, Willi, *The Developing Child: Sense and Nonsense in Education,* Great Barrington, MA: Anthroposophic Press, 2001.

Barteges, Carol Anne & Nick Lyons, *Educating As an Art: Essays on Waldorf Education,* New York: Rudolf Steiner School NYC, 2003.

Clouder, Christopher, & Martyn Rawson, *Waldorf Education,* Edinburgh: Floris Books, 2003.

Finser, Torin M., *In Search of Ethical Leadership: If not now, when?* Great Barrington, MA: SteinerBooks, 2003.

———, *School As a Journey: The Eight-Year Odyssey of a Waldorf Teacher and His Class,* Great Barrington, MA: Anthroposophic Press, 1994.

———, *School Renewal: A Spiritual Journey for Change,* Great Barrington, MA: Anthroposophic Press, 2001.

Harwood, A. C., *The Recovery of Man in Childhood: A Study of the Educational Work of Rudolf Steiner,* Great Barrington, MA: The Myrin Institute, 2001.

———, *The Way of a Child: An Introduction to the Work of Rudolf Steiner for Children,* London, Rudolf Steiner Press, 1967.

Jaffke, Freya, *Work and Play in Early Childhood,* Great Barrington, MA: Anthroposophic Press, 1991.

Nobel, Agnes, *Educating through Art: The Steiner School Approach,* Edinburgh: Floris Books, 1996.

Peck, Betty, *Kindergarten Education: Freeing Children's Creative Potential,* Stroud, UK: Hawthorn Press, 2004.

Schwartz, Eugene, *Millennial Child: Transforming Education in the Twenty-First Century,* Great Barrington, MA: Anthroposophic Press, 1999.

Spock, Marjorie, *Teaching As a Lively Art,* Great Barrington, MA: SteinerBooks, 2003.

Trostli, Roberto, & Rudolf Steiner. *Rhythms of Learning: What Waldorf Education Offers Children, Parents & Teachers,* Great Barrington, MA: Anthroposophic Press, 1998.

INDEX

Waldorf education
>basis for, 4–5, 46–47
>coeducational, 3
>dealing with modern life, 3–4
>difficulty of discussing, 89
>foundations of, 225–26
>goals and principles of, 18, 24, 157–58, 160, 202

Waldorf school
>block teaching, 149–50
>coeducational approach, 3, 185–86, 199–200
>as complete organism, 191–92
>grouping children by temperament, 173–74
>teachers' meetings, 198–99, 200
>teachers' seminar, 77
>valuing artistic education for early years, 109

walking, 68, 91–95, 178–79

Western civilization, development of, 43

will
>bringing word into, 80–82
>freed through movement, 75
>released from organism, 70–71, 73–74

wisdom, from revelation and *inspiration*, 41

women, place in Greek civilization, 40

word (*Logos*), 80–86

work, aesthetics in, 102

wrestling, 28–29, 31

writing, 108, 121–23, 125, 141, 180

Z

zither, 30, 31

Millennial Child

EUGENE SCHWARTZ

In assuming that children can assimilate a conceptual framework that was once considered fit only for adults, we have indeed turned children into "little adults" who (it would appear) can think logically, make decisions for themselves, and express precocious sexual desires. (Eugene Schwartz)

Today's children are an endangered species. Schwartz presents an incisive analysis of how the errors of the previous century have returned to haunt us. After carefully examining Freud's tragic misunderstanding of childhood and its consequences for parents and educators, the author points to the radically new paradigm of childhood development offered by Waldorf education. Parents, teachers, and child psychologists will find a wealth of insight into such subjects as the nature of play, the causes of ADHD, computers as teachers, and the power that love and imagination have in educating the "millennial child."

320 pages, paperback
ISBN 0-88010-465-1
$19.95

The Spiritual Ground of Education

RUDOLF STEINER

9 Lectures, Manchester College, Oxford, England, Aug. 16–29, 1922 (GA 305)

Given during a conference on spiritual values in education and life attended by many prominent people of the time, Steiner's Oxford lectures gave him a rare opportunity to present the principles of Waldorf education at the highest cultural level. According to *The Manchester Guardian:*

Dr. Steiner's lectures, for which we express our very special thanks, brought to us in a very vivid way an ideal of humanity in education. He spoke to us about teachers who, freely and unitedly, unrestricted by external prescription, develop their educational methods exclusively out of a thorough knowledge of human nature. He spoke to us about a kind of knowledge needed by the teacher, a knowledge of the being of man and of the world, which is at the same time scientific and also penetrates into the most intimate inner life, which is intuitive and artistic.

These lectures—the first of three courses to English audiences—constitute one of the best introductions to Waldorf education.

164 pages, paperback
ISBN 0-88010-513-5
$20.00

Living Alphabet

FAMKE ZONNEVELD

Afterword by William Ward

In this delightful picture-alphabet game book for young children, each consonant and vowel comes alive with its own unique qualities in the world. A Cat naps on a carpet conjuring cows and conch shells, clocks and crows, cubes and columns; a Girl gives grain to geese in a gated garden, watched over by giraffes and grasshoppers, gondolas and grapes, gourds and a geodesic globe. Mermaids muse in the moonlight under mountains surrounded by monkeys and moose, minarets and mice, mosquitoes and a menorah. *(Ages 4–6)*

FAMKE ZONNEVELD is an artist and art teacher. She taught crafts and the history of architecture at the Rudolf Steiner School in New York City. She studied Goethe's color theories with Donald Hall, a student of Beppe Assensa. She lives and works in western Massachusetts.

60 pages, hardcover
ISBN 0-88010-516-X
$19.95

Mr. Goethe's Garden

DIANA COHN

Illustrated by Paul Mirocha

This is the story of friendship between an inquisitive young girl and her elderly neighbor, the famous playwright, artist, and scientist Johann von Goethe. Set in the 1830s, the girl visits Mr. Goethe in his garden, where she is taught to draw and to see the world of nature in a very special way.

Inspired by Goethe's life and his botanical treatise *The Metamorphosis of the Plant,* this book contains exquisite, sensitive illustrations and elegant text that reveal the intricate wonders of the plant kingdom. As the bonds of friendship between the girl and her wise, kindly neighbor grow stronger, young readers experience with her a new way of seeing the natural cycle of the plant—from seed to flower to fruit and to seed again.

An informative afterword describes the life of Goethe and his many accomplishments. *(Ages 7–9)*

DIANA COHN is an educator committed to social justice work. She has a master's degree in education from Teacher's College, Columbia University.

32 pages, hardcover
ISBN 0-88010-521-6
$17.95

What Is Waldorf Education?
Three Lectures

RUDOLF STEINER

Introduction by Stephen Sagarin

This is a reader-friendly "taster" of three public lectures on Waldorf education, with a thought-provoking introduction by a teacher and longtime student of Waldorf education. The lectures present the fundamentals of Steiner's educational methods in a matter-of-fact, objective, and non-dogmatic way. The wide-ranging, informative introduction addresses Waldorf education and methodology in general, explaining that, before all else, a Waldorf school is a *good* school. This is a must-read for anyone involved with or interested in Waldorf education.

128 pages, paperback
ISBN 0-88010-527-5
$12.00

What Is Anthroposophy?
Three Spiritual Perspectives on Self-Knowledge

RUDOLF STEINER

3 lectures, July 20–22, 1923, Dornach (GA 225)
Introduced by Christopher Bamford
Translated by Mado Spiegler

These three previously untranslated lectures are a masterly introduction to Rudolf Steiner and anthroposophy. They explain why this path "unites what is spiritual in the human being with what is spiritual in the universe."

Steiner describes what happens when we die, showing the relationship between physical life on Earth and the etheric, astral, and spiritual life of the cosmos. He explains how our physical lives are completely interwoven with cosmic existence, and how the "missing links" in evolution are spiritual in nature. He demonstrates the shallow soullessness of mainstream psychology and points out that the idea of the soul has been lost.

Using our three states of being—waking, dreaming, and sleeping—as his guide, Steiner describes these conditions and how each is connected with our lives as physical, psychic, and spiritual beings.

The profound insights in this book make the world a larger, richer, and more exciting place.

96 pages, paperback
ISBN 0-88010-506-2
$9.95

DURING THE LAST TWO DECADES of the nineteenth
century the Austrian-born Rudolf Steiner (1861–1925)
became a respected and well-published scientific, literary,
and philosophical scholar, particularly known for his work
on Goethe's scientific writings. After the turn of the century,
he began to develop his earlier philosophical principles into a
methodical approach to the research of psychological and
spiritual phenomena.

His multifaceted genius led to innovative and holistic
approaches in medicine, science, education (Waldorf
schools), special education, philosophy, religion, agriculture
(biodynamic farming), architecture, drama, movement
(eurythmy), speech, and other fields. In 1924 he founded the
General Anthroposophical Society, which has branches
throughout the world.

Printed in the United States
16638LVS00002B/1-57

9 780880 105118